THE BROWNINGS
OF CASA GUIDI

BOOKS BY EDWARD C. MCALEER

Dearest Isa: Robert Browning's Letters to Isabella Blagden

The Sensitive Plant: A Life of Lady Mount Cashell

Learned Lady: Letters from Robert Browning to Mrs. Thomas FitzGerald

The Brownings of Casa Guidi

THE BROWNINGS
OF CASA GUIDI

BY

EDWARD C. McALEER

THE BROWNING INSTITUTE, INC.

NEW YORK

© Copyright 1979 The Browning Institute, Inc.

Library of Congress Catalog Card Number: 78–56858

ISBN 0–930252–04–7 *cloth binding*
ISBN 0–930252–03–9 *paperback*

First published 1979
Second printing (with revisions) 1984
Third printing 1987

Manufactured in the United States of America

The Browning Institute, Inc. was founded in 1971 to acquire the apartment in Casa Guidi, Florence, which had been the home of Robert and Elizabeth Barrett Browning. The Institute has preserved the apartment as a memorial to the two poets and has opened it to visitors without charge.

You are invited to become a member of The Browning Institute. Inquiries should be sent to The Treasurer, The Browning Institute, Inc., Box 2983, Grand Central Station, New York, N.Y. 10163. The Institute is a nonprofit organization chartered in the State of New York, and dues and contributions are tax-deductible. A copy of the latest annual report of the Institute may be obtained upon request by writing to the Office of Charities Registration, New York State Department of State, 162 Washington Avenue, Albany, N.Y. 12231, or to The Browning Institute at the address above.

The address of Casa Guidi is Piazza San Felice 8, 50125 Firenze, Italy.

CONTENTS

ILLUSTRATIONS

Numerals in the margins of the text refer the reader to illustrations.

FOREWORD

This is a guidebook to Casa Guidi, the Florentine home of Robert and Elizabeth Barrett Browning. It is a guide to the Brownings' home and to the Brownings at home. Although they earned their places in English literary history first as poets and then as "immortal lovers," in this book they are presented as a man and woman, a husband and wife, and a father and mother. Unlike most of us, they wrote poetry that has lasted, and their courtship has inspired *The Barretts of Wimpole Street*, Rudolf Besier's successful play and motion picture. Like most of us, however, they devoted much of their time to getting and spending and to such commonplace activities as buying used furniture, shopping for clothes, submitting to the dentist, and supervising their son's piano lessons. I have selected everyday details of this sort from their letters and the writings of their contemporaries to present the Brownings to the common reader in a sort of prose sequel to the Besier play.

I have seen this play at home and abroad and even in Caserta, Italy, where Katherine Cornell contributed her fine production to the war effort. Always the audience has sat riveted through the play and then, with applause and curtain calls and unqualified good wishes, has sent the lovers from Wimpole Street to Paris. It is pleasant now in this sequel to tell the audiences that their wishes were granted off-stage and that for fifteen years the Brownings lived a married life with as much happiness as poets and mortal lovers are allowed.

The reader who wishes to learn more about the poets and their work might well begin with G. K. Chesterton's *Robert Browning* (1903) and Alethea Hayter's *Mrs. Browning: A Poet's Work and Its Setting* (1962). The current standard biographies are William Irvine and Park Honan's *The Book, the Ring, & the Poet: A Biography of Robert Browning* (1974), Donald Thomas's *Robert Browning* (1982), Gardner B. Taplin's *The Life of Elizabeth Barrett Browning* (1957), and Maisie Ward's *The Tragi-Comedy of Pen Browning* (1972).

Giuliana Artom Treves's *Anglo-Fiorentini di Cento Anni Fa* (1953), translated into English as *The Golden Ring*, is an Italian woman's account of the Brownings' circle in Florence; and Francis Steegmuller's *The Two Lives of James Jackson Jarves* (1951) is an account of an American art collector who was a resident of Florence in the Brownings' day. Mrs. Artom and Mr. Steegmuller have read this book in typescript, and I am grateful for their observations.

Especially do I thank Frank Arroyo, Robert Best, the late Count Alberto Guidi, Philip Kelley, and Arthur Sweeny, Jr., who supplied information and helped with the illustrations.

Quotations from the Brownings' correspondence are used with the kind permission of John Murray.

Permission to quote from Mrs. Browning's unpublished letters to her sister Arabel and to Sophia Eckley has been granted by the Henry W. and Albert A. Berg Collection of the New York Public Library, Astor, Lenox, and Tilden Foundations.

New York City   EDWARD C. MCALEER

THE BROWNINGS
OF CASA GUIDI

THE BROWNINGS

Robert and Elizabeth Barrett Browning are today associated with Florence and Casa Guidi, but they had not originally intended to make their home there. On the contrary, during their courtship Robert had opposed Florence as a residence because the city was "inhabited by hordes of vulgar and pushing English, *parvenus* who would have been inexorably excluded from polite society in England." Browning knew first hand, having been twice to Italy before his marriage and having observed the resident English in Pisa and Florence. But the couple went to Florence for a visit, fell in love with the beauty and "celestial cheapness" of the city, and made it their headquarters for the remaining years of their married life. "Headquarters" is a fitting word, for they were away from Florence about half the time. Of the fifteen winters they lived together, seven were spent in Pisa or Paris or Rome; and eleven of their summers were spent, at least in part, in London or Siena or at the Bagni di Lucca or the Havre. Yet they were always happy to return to their own chairs and tables, books and pictures, and to the dear Tuscan language. "Florence is my chimney corner where I can sulk and be happy," Elizabeth said. It was there that Elizabeth gave birth to her son, there that she died, and there that Robert said his heart was buried.

London to Pisa
September 19 to October 14, 1846

The Brownings had been married seven months when they first arrived in Florence. On September 12, 1846, without letting her father, eight brothers, or sisters Henrietta and Arabel know,

Elizabeth and her maid had slipped out of the Barretts' London house on Wimpole Street and had met Robert in the parish church. The maid, a necessary accessory, had been told about the plan only the night before. After the wedding, the couple separated and did not meet again for a week, when they "eloped" to Paris.

The honeymoon party consisted of the forty-year-old bride, her thirty-four-year-old bridegroom, her maid Wilson, and her cocker spaniel, Flush. Like many persons of genius, the poets were of less than average size. Elizabeth seemed no bigger than a doll, and, because her brother "Bro" thought her only half the size of a baby, he gave her the nickname "Ba," which was the first syllable of the word *ba-by* and came to be pronounced *bah*. Thomas Bailey Aldrich met Robert three times and said of him, "Good head, long body, short legs. Seated, he looked like a giant; standing he just missed being a dwarf." (Still, at five feet four, Robert was somewhat taller than John Keats and much taller than Queen Victoria.) Their fellow poet D. G. Rossetti considered them one of his "delights" during their first return visit to London, and he wondered as they were on their way back to Italy, "How large a part of the real world . . . are those two small people? – taking meanwhile so little room in any railway carriage, and hardly needing a double bed at the inn." Maid Elizabeth Wilson was a young Yorkshire woman as tiny as her mistress.

Once in Paris, Robert immediately alerted Elizabeth's friend Anna Murphy Jameson. They rested a week, and Mrs. Jameson, efficiently in charge, got them south to Marseilles by railroad, steamer, and carriage, then on board ship to Genoa and Leghorn, thence twelve miles overland to Pisa, where she saw them established in furnished rooms in the Collegio di Ferdinando, close to the Duomo. The voyage was tiring, of course, because Elizabeth was an invalid.

Pisa
October 14, 1846 to April 20, 1847

They remained six months in Pisa, Elizabeth dividing her time between the bedroom and the sitting room. By night she slept well on the "most uncomfortable of beds . . . stuffed with orange shavings," and by day Robert left his post beside her chair only when she drove him out for "his hour's solitary exercise." Mornings found them by the sitting-room fire at breakfast of eggs, toasted rolls, and coffee. Evenings found them roasting chestnuts and eating grapes by the same fire of pine wood.

Delicious hot meals costing next to nothing were sent in from a *trattoria*. At two-o'clock dinner, Robert *would* keep pouring chianti into her tumbler whenever she looked the other way. At the end of the meal, when she was "too giddy to see his face," he would stretch her out full length in the arm chair, and at his command she would go to sleep. (The "unutterably" happy Robert was trying to wean her from the morphine that her London physicians had prescribed, and indeed she was using less and less.) After they ate, Wilson would have her own dinner and tumbler of chianti. Elizabeth's only household duty was to sit at the table and make coffee with the ingredients Wilson had fetched. In later years Elizabeth boasted that in all her married life she had never once had to order a meal.

They did not need the society of the resident English. Their decision was to "cut everybody" and see nobody. When Mrs. Stisted, an endearingly eccentric lion hunter, threatened to call, Elizabeth instructed Wilson not to admit her, and Robert begged his wife not to receive that "coarse, vulgar, pushing" Mrs. Trollope. "These people will spoil our happiness," he said, "if we once let them in." Instead they kept to themselves and talked merry nonsense. We have "been nowhere," Elizabeth wrote to her sister. We "never see a creature." That was the life she preferred. Especially she enjoyed "leaving the world and above all oneself" with the help of novels. She would rather communicate in writing than in person. At one point during her courtship, Robert had been more real to her in his letters than in the flesh, even after he had declared his love. Years earlier, when her father planned to sell Hope End, their big country house, and move elsewhere, Elizabeth wrote in her diary, "I will seclude myself . . . & try to know & like nobody – but live with my books & writings & dear family." Often she thought that the life of a Trappist monk in perpetual silence would suit her perfectly.

From a circulating library Robert brought home books by the dozen, scolding Elizabeth for reading those "wicked" French novels by the prolific Eugène Sue, but he kept bringing them home, and she kept reading them. Much as she deplored the lack of "delicacy" in the novels of Paul de Kock, she overcame her distaste and managed to get through more than thirty of them from cover to cover. (Molly Bloom in James Joyce's *Ulysses* was a later Victorian who used to lie in bed titillated by the same writer's books fetched by an indulgent husband.) Later, Robert made strange use of his wife's addiction to French romances. In *Men and Women*, he had his Bishop Blougram observe:

> Our interest's on the dangerous edge of things.
> The honest thief, the tender murderer,
> The superstitious atheist, demireps
> That love and save their souls in new French books –

Thus they lived, Elizabeth writing that she was happier than she ever had been in her life, finding it strange and delightful that Robert loved her "with increase." He assured her that his love grew stronger and, as he had kissed her feet before their marriage, he would now kiss the ground under her feet.

Invalids Abroad
1847

In January Wilson gave Elizabeth an awful fright. Elizabeth was sitting before the fire late at night, undressed. She was just putting her feet into the hot bath water when Wilson sank down on the sofa "in a shivering fit," crying out that she was going to be very ill. Elizabeth dried her own feet, put on a dressing gown, and tried to get Wilson to go out to Dr. Cook. The "signorina of the household" (the landlady's daughter) refused to accompany

Wilson lest she faint on the way. Then Elizabeth sent Wilson to bed with fever and beating pulse, and asked Robert to get dressed and summon the doctor. Robert had some objections, but he went.

It was only then that Elizabeth learned that Wilson had been silently suffering with a distended stomach for four months and had been doctoring herself with English pills. A week previously she had mentioned a pain in the left side, for which she was taking calomel, rhubarb, cream of tartar, and herb water. (Robert was critical of "such redundancy of medicine.") Dr. Cook arrived, professionally calm. Wilson had "a slight inflammation of the mucous membrane." The doctor, who tended to embellish his diagnoses with *if's*, said, "If the symptoms had continued. . . . If the inflammation had extended to the bowels. . . ." He confined Wilson to bed with five leeches on her side and forbade coffee and the tumblers of chianti. Elizabeth had no doubt that the cause was seasickness, although Wilson had not been on the sea for months.

Then Robert turned on Elizabeth – not because he had to get dressed and race across Pisa after ten o'clock, but because Elizabeth had risked her own health by running to Wilson's room "without any stockings." He thought that the reckless Elizabeth "wanted to kill him" and "played with his life." As if, she said, anybody catches cold "in such a fright." She thought it just too much that if her foot went to sleep Robert got a headache. During Wilson's illness, Elizabeth had to comb her own hair and dress herself, lacing stays and reconciling hooks and eyes without assistance. Robert's concern for his wife's health was not exaggerated or unwarranted.

Elizabeth's health merits comment. She was the first of twelve children and an indulged, precocious child. She was also something of a tomboy given to fisticuffs, strenuous activity, and to throwing things about the house. When she was fifteen, she underwent a prolonged illness, diagnosed then as a "nervous disorder." She had been unusually close to her brother Bro, who was one year her junior and resembled her. They had been baptized together and had played together, fought together, and studied Latin and Greek together until he left Hope End for Charterhouse, his public school. During the "agony" of his absence, Elizabeth wrote her "Verses to My Brother" and suffered her first "nervous disorder." She felt the effects for at least a year.

Sixteen years later, when she was thirty-one, she neglected a cough and "broke a blood vessel." For years thereafter she suffered irregular heart beat, blood-spitting, loss of voice, fever, fainting spells, and insomnia. Her doctors, who diagnosed congested lungs, prescribed opium in the form of morphine taken orally and laudanum. When she first met Robert she was living in an upstairs bedroom and taking forty drops of laudanum a day, more than six times an average prescription now. (Victorian physicians prescribed with less sophisticated caution than do physicians today.) Medical opinion in our time thinks she may have had a "general tuberculosis from girlhood." Those who wear Freudian spectacles see malingering for the amenities of invalidism. Certainly the symptoms were real.

In January, when Dr. Cook was visiting Wilson, he had expressed delight at the "manifold improvement" in Elizabeth's appearance, which he attributed to the Pisan air. In early March, she wrote that she was "well and happy" and walked "as in a dream." However, at four in the morning of Sunday, March 21, Elizabeth had a miscarriage – the first of four – after five months' pregnancy. For a few weeks she had suspected that something was wrong with her, but could have sworn that she had just "caught cold." Only Wilson had silently suspected the truth. When she finally spoke, she said that the pains were "not right" and that she had "great fears about the influence of the *morphine*." On Saturday evening regular pains came on every five minutes and recurred for above twenty-four hours. After the crisis, Dr. Cook said that "If he had been called in six weeks ago . . . ." He did not blame the morphine. Rather, he proscribed the chianti and prescribed port. Readmitted to the sick room after the event, Robert took it harder than did Elizabeth, throwing "himself down on the bed in a passion of tears, sobbing like a child." Elizabeth's recovery was remarkable and without special medication except for the leeches attached to her back. After three days, she was able to get up for an hour and then for progressively longer periods.

In the course of the six months in Pisa, they did do some sightseeing, visiting a few churches and taking a few carriage rides to the sea and to the pine woods. Sometimes Elizabeth was strong enough to go for short walks and to church. How she objected to the "imbecility and inconsequence" of the English preacher who held forth to the pink bonnets and the blue bonnets who had paid a shilling each for admission to the services he conducted in a "mere room." Preferable were midnight mass in the cathedral at Christmas and the hour-long Lenten sermons of an eloquent Catholic friar. Although there was much left unseen in Pisa, their lease was up on April 17, and they had agreed to meet Mrs. Jameson in Florence on the twenty-fourth. Before leaving, Elizabeth with her own hand cut off Robert's mustachios.

Florence
April 20 to July 14, 1847

They had considered hiring a *vettura* (a private carriage) for the journey, but at the last minute they decided to engage the coupé in the diligence (public stagecoach) that was to take them the sixty odd miles from Pisa to Florence, where they arrived on Tuesday, April 20. There was a good deal of shaking in the diligence, and Elizabeth lay half the time across Robert's knees. The diligence sped rapidly across one of the bridges over the "old dear yellow Arno" and drew up before the door of the Hotel du Nord. Robert carried Elizabeth into the hotel and placed her on a sofa. On Wednesday, he went out looking for an apartment. On Thursday, Robert, Elizabeth, Wilson, and Flush moved into furnished rooms at 4222 Via delle Belle Donne, just off the Piazza Santa Maria Novella. The lease was for two months at £4 a month and later was extended for another month until July 22.

The apartment was perfect. The rent included linen, plate, china, decanters, and champagne glasses. There was even a spring sofa for Elizabeth and bell pulls to summon Wilson. (At

Pisa Elizabeth had had to rent a sofa and to ask Robert to get up and knock on a door whenever she needed her maid.) At her urging, Robert rented a grand piano of German make which, with the hire of music, cost ten shillings a month. For six shillings a month a charwoman came in daily to make the beds, clean the rooms, and brush Robert's clothes. Wilson was pleased with the superior elegance. "*It is something like*," she said.

The *trattoria* nearby was even better than the one in Pisa. For two shillings and eight pence a day and without the bother of Robert's having to order, dinners for three were sent in at three o'clock: soup, three entrées, vegetables, and a pudding or tart. Elizabeth described a typical meal of vermicelli, sturgeon, turkey, stewed beef, mashed potatoes, and cheese cakes. There were always leftovers for supper. Wine, of course, was extra. Robert, who would not touch the port the doctor had prescribed for Elizabeth, paid three pence a bottle for his wine. Elizabeth's only, slight regret was that Robert did not know how to carve.

After dinner Robert would put Elizabeth in a great arm chair, rub eau de cologne on her hands and forehead, and fan her until her eyes closed in sleep. After their supper at seven-thirty, the couple would walk on the terrace in the cool of the evening. Then Elizabeth would lie on the sofa, and Robert would play to her on the rented pianoforte. They were in bed by ten or ten-thirty.

On Friday the twenty-third, in the gloaming, Elizabeth was lying on the sofa as Robert played "A Light of Love," said by some musicologist to have been Shakespeare's favorite air. The door opened and in came Mrs. Jameson. "Upon my word," she said, "here's domestic harmony!" She had remembered that it was Shakespeare's birthday and had come from Rome a day early with a bottle of wine from Arezzo to drink a toast with the two poets. She and her niece, who was travelling with her, took coffee and supper with the Brownings, who engaged an additional bedroom for them. She thought that Elizabeth looked very well "considering," that Robert was still that "inexhaustible man," and that Elizabeth was reproachable for having cut off his mustachios.

Mrs. Jameson was an art historian gathering material for her forthcoming *Sacred and Legendary Art*. Elizabeth was not yet strong enough to visit the galleries with her during the week she stayed in Florence, but a fortnight later, in mid-May, Elizabeth took her first "glorious" drive around the Piazza del Granduca, thence outside the city walls, and back again through the Cascine, where, as is well known, Shelley wrote his "Ode to the West Wind." Robert was in raptures when she left the carriage and walked by herself. She thought Florence "the most beautiful of cities devised by man."

Gradually they were able to do more. They went about, sat on the bridge, and would even "after the vulgarest fashion" take an ice inside Doney's Café. They viewed the "divine" art in the Uffizi and Pitti galleries. At home they read together Vasari's *Lives of the Painters*, and Elizabeth continued reading her novels and listening to Robert's music. They avoided the English colony, of course, but they did make the effort to attend one reception in order to meet Mr. and Mrs. Richard B. Hoppner, who had once "seen Shelley plain" in Venice. (The Brownings did not know that the Shelleys had come to despise the Hoppners as scandalous gossips.) On carriage drives, Elizabeth would protect herself from the late afternoon sun with a parasol. On one of these drives they saluted the Grand Duke in his carriage, and graciously he took off his hat to them "in the sun." But they were on their way "to see higher dignities" – in the villa where Milton said he had visited Galileo.

Flush endured the adaptation to Continental life. On the train from Paris the "barbarians" had confined him in a box; in Pisa he was insolent to other dogs; and in Florence he became very ill with spasms and fits of screaming. They gave him castor oil and tied him with a rope round his neck near a mat provided in the kitchen. Flush survived, but still had before him the frightful fleas of his first summer in Tuscany.

A Marriage Settlement
May 1847

Early in May arrived a box with "precious deeds." Three weeks later Fanny Hanford and her brother, friends of John Kenyon, spent a day in Florence, witnessed the Brownings' signatures, and then took the deeds to Mr. Kenyon in England. This was the "marriage settlement."

John Kenyon was a schoolmate of Robert's father, a poet, and rich. It was through him that the poets had met. At the time of the marriage, Robert was penniless and had to borrow £100 from his father for the honeymoon. Elizabeth also borrowed: £70 from her sister Arabel and £55 from Mrs. Minny Robinson, the housekeeper. Elizabeth was better off than Robert, having inherited £8,000 from her grandmother Moulton and her uncle Sam Barrett. This sum was invested in government bonds and produced after taxes £180 a year. She also owned shares in one of her father's trading ships, the *David Lyon*, which had been known to provide her with £200 a year but more often with much less or nothing. In addition she could expect royalties from her poetry. During her first married year she received £25 from *Blackwood's* magazine for some sonnets and £75 from her publisher Moxon. For many years, even long after her death, her poetry brought in more than Robert's.

According to law, when she signed the marriage document, Robert fell into "unrestricted possession" of her fortune. It is not surprising then that people, including her father and brothers, thought that he had married for money. Kenyon offered to manage the poets' finances and went further by asking them to draw on him if they were in need. He recommended the marriage settlement and two of Robert's friends as trustees. The legal process was distasteful. Neither signer read the document, but Elizabeth did note that provision was made for her progeny and "future husbands!!" The settlement tied Robert's hands, but it stopped the gossips' tongues. Robert served champagne. The next step was for Elizabeth to make her will, designating Robert sole executor, as Mr. Kenyon had suggested.

This difference in their resources accounts for the dissimilarity in their attitudes towards money. Elizabeth, daughter of gentry, would spend more than she had and not think of being in debt. Robert, son of a bank clerk, was under compulsion to spend less than he possessed and to budget for unforeseen emergencies. She thought it "morbid" of him to fuss so about paying bills when they were due, and she smiled at his recording every spent farthing in his little black account books, some of which are extant. (He remained cautious and "unpoetical" until his death. It is today possible to go to the British Library, fill out a call slip, and read in Robert's handwriting how much he tipped the coachman who drove him to the Royal Academy on Thursday, January 4, 1883.) Elizabeth did not keep account books, but she transmitted the price of just about everything to her correspondents.

Leaves in Vallombrosa
July 14 to 19, 1847

A week before their lease ran out, the thermometer registered 85 degrees, and Elizabeth longed for the cool of the mountains. Robert suggested several places nearby where they might go, but she had set her heart upon Vallombrosa, the Benedictine monastery founded in 1015, where women had never been welcome. She displayed what T. A. Trollope called the "incomprehensible mania of female English heretics" to visit male monasteries. They had secured a letter from the Archbishop of Florence to the Abbot, who she was sure would grant her and Wilson dispensation. On Wednesday, July 14, they rose at three in the morning and at four began the thirteen-mile drive along the Arno to Pelago, where they ate at the inn. Then she, Wilson, Flush, and the luggage were put into two old wine baskets, without wheels, each basket attached to two white bullocks. The luggage included a dozen bottles of medicinal port for Elizabeth. For five hours they were dragged the four miles up the mountain, Robert pacing up and down the precipitous paths on horseback. It was cold on the mountain, and Elizabeth and Wilson put on their flannel petticoats as soon as Wilson unpacked.

Elizabeth was accustomed to have her own way, but at Vallombrosa the aristocratic Abbot was accustomed to have his. The women were allowed to stay the licit three days in an external guest house. The scenery with pines and waterfalls was "magnificent," the bread "fetid," and the Abbot unbrowbeatable. Despite Robert's "eloquent amiability" and "unprecedented subservience," the women were not welcome. "Those idiots of monks" told them to leave. For another day they fought back, but had to leave on the fifth, Elizabeth bitter and angry. In jest she wrote to Fanny Dowglass that it gave her "a malign satisfaction" to put foot over the threshold and stamp thrice on the monks' ground, "profaning it for ever." So on Monday the heretics rose at three in the morning, and with Elizabeth and Wilson and the port packed in the wine hampers, slid down the precipitous paths through the glorious scenery to Florence, their old lodgings, and the heat. Fortunately, their lease was good for two more days.

Casa Guidi
July 20 to October 19, 1847

Delightful as the lodgings had been through the winter, they were now in July unbearably hot. "Poor dearest Robert" hunted for another place, returning "in despair" and "white with exhaustion" before he found furnished rooms in the Casa Guidi on the Via Maggio close to the Pitti Palace. The rooms were on the *piano nobile*, large and cool, and the Guidi family furniture was fit for their predecessor, a Russian prince. The amenities included two terraces and daily admission (Flush excluded) to the Boboli gardens. Robert took the rooms for two months at a guinea a week, remarkably cheap because it was the "dead part of the season."

They rehired the grand piano and renewed their subscription to the Vieusseux circulating library and newsroom. The heat was bearable in the airy rooms, where the sun never came "except for a side glance," and Robert let Elizabeth sit all day in her white dressing gown. They lived on fruit, including figs, grapes, and watermelon that Wilson had lowered into the well in Casa

Guidi and thus cooled. At six every evening a little breeze moved the curtains on the great windows. After coffee at seven-thirty, they walked side by side on the terrace until the moon rose. The blank walls of San Felice church opposite the terrace meant that they could not be observed from windows, allowing Elizabeth to walk outdoors without her bonnet. If she tired, she could sink into a chair in one of the windows that opened on the terrace, which was so narrow that Flush would venture by himself or with Elizabeth but not *à trois*.

No "vulgar, pushing" Anglo-Florentines pushed across the Guidi threshold. One privileged visitor was Mary Boyle, Irish and a poet. Her credentials were impeccable. Her uncle was the Earl of Cork, her mother was Lady Boyle, and her aunt "the Queen Dowager's maid of honor." Robert had once met her at Lady Morgan's where, he said, she was "crème de la crème" in London society. The Boyles had been in Florence for four months, staying in the Villa Careggi, which had been lent them by Lord Holland and where Lorenzo the Magnificent had lived and died. Miss Boyle had sent a letter and Elizabeth had replied, saying that she would receive her.

Her first call was embarrassing. Wilson and Annunziata, the second maid, were out, and Robert had to answer the door himself, "*en déshabille*," that is to say, "without his necktie." With the manners of an aristocrat, Miss Boyle "condescended" to say, "Oh, you ought to see me and my sister in the morning." She called often during the following months, arriving after supper, staying for chestnuts roasted on a brazier, mulled wine, and conversation until eleven or twelve. Robert and she talked vivaciously as Elizabeth listened. "A lively little aristocrat," said Robert.

Receiving Miss Boyle was one thing, but going out of an evening to see her in private theatricals was another. In the spring she acted in an amateur play at the villa of Charles Lever (another Irish writer), and she and Elizabeth pressed Robert to attend. He was not to be persuaded, being "far happier at home" with his wife.

Festa
September 12, 1847

They enjoyed celebrating the day of their marriage, at first once a week on Saturdays, then once a month on the twelfth. September 12, 1847, was their first anniversary, and they planned especial observance. The Italians unwittingly cooperated. In 1847 Tuscany was still under Austrian rule, and the Grand Duke, Leopold II, who lived in the palace across the square, was not of an Italian house but of Hapsburg-Lorraine. Loveable despot though he was, the Brownings would prefer an independent and united Italy. One concession made that year was that the Grand Duke granted the Tuscans a civic guard, and some forty thousand enthusiasts assembled to rejoice.

The Brownings watched from a window of their building, Elizabeth "enthroned on cushions" on a chair. She, Robert, Miss Boyle, and Flush saw it all – the Grand Duke at his window, the three-and-a-half-hour procession in the day. On her evening walk to the Arno to see the illuminations, Elizabeth noted with approval the lack of drunkenness, brutality, fist-fighting, and blasphemous language regrettably inevitable in an English crowd. For days her wrist ached from fluttering her handkerchief at the window.

There was one unpleasantness: Flush stayed out all night. He had seemed bored and fidgety during the long vigil at the window with his paws on the sill. When Annunziata took him out for his walk, Robert being ill, he ran away and refused to be traced, even by Robert, who, ill though he was, dressed and stalked his wife's dog through the festive crowds in the piazza. The porter left the street door open until midnight, but Flush remained truant. Elizabeth was distracted, more so because he had been kidnapped and ransomed more than once in London. In the morning, he returned looking guilty and bedraggled, "as if he had been running about all night." (When cold weather came, Flush was content to lie by the fire eating "bunch after bunch" of grapes.)

They had been making plans to move on to Rome about September 20, when their lease would terminate, especially because the winter rent in Casa Guidi would be double what they were paying. Elizabeth's poor health helped them to decide to remain in Florence, and they extended their lease a bit. Robert and the *padrone* of the *casa* haggled over the rent, and the *padrone* came down to within shillings of Robert's offer, but the adamant poet took his lares and penates and his account book elsewhere.

He could neither eat nor sleep as he went from one side of Florence to the other finding apartments that Elizabeth would then reject. Having developed a "taste for *festas*," she *did* want a window from which she could observe the gaiety.

Ten Sunless Days
October 19 to [29?], 1847

At 1881 Via Maggio, they took rooms formerly occupied by the Princess of Würtemburg of the House of Brunswick. Robert signed for six months at five pounds six a month. Elizabeth liked the apartment, especially her own "faultless" room, the one in which the princess had given birth. There was a *chaise longue*, but no terrace. Very soon they learned that there was no sunshine. Within ten days they knew they must move elsewhere. It was vexing to have to commit themselves to pay rent for two residences. In her letters Elizabeth took the blame for "being abominable," and Robert took the blame in his.

Piazza Pitti Windows
October [29?], 1847 to May 9, 1848

At last they found the perfect location in the Piazza Pitti precisely opposite the Grand Duke, though the flat seemed a "doll's house" after the tall chambers of Casa Guidi. They signed another lease. (How provoking it was to learn that after they had left Casa Guidi the agent was prepared to accept their terms!) However, they now had five windows that looked out on the festivity of the square.

> One, he carries a flag up straight, and another a cross
> with handles,

And the Duke's guard brings up the rear, for the better
    prevention of scandals.
Bang-whang-whang goes the drum, *tootle-te-tootle* the
    fife.
Oh, a day in the city-square, there is no such pleasure in
    life!

Thus wrote Robert in "Up at a Villa – Down in the City," published eight years later.

The rooms had sunshine from morning till night. Elizabeth went often for twenty-minute walks in the piazza and sometimes visited the gallery to "adore" the Raphaels. Their rooms had "festa day advantages" with full view of the civic guard parading and the crowds watching. Robert had not left her alone a single evening since their marriage, and she could not make him go out even for two hours to a concert or a play, both of which he loved. Books and music and small talk made the "clock gallop."

They were poets who wrote no poetry. Robert was not a compulsive writer like, say, William Faulkner or William Blake. No demon drove his pen at any hour of the day or night. During the first year of his marriage he wrote to Miss Haworth, "I could, with an unutterably easy heart, never write another line while I have my being." Later, in Rome, he would spend hours at sculpture or painting in the studios of friends, "neglecting his own art." In these Florentine days, he seems to have done no more than revise earlier work in the midst of "daylong blessed idleness."

Elizabeth loved to write her long, delightful letters as Robert marvelled at the quick, tiny fingers flying over the page. "Tell me everything you want to know," she wrote to a friend. "I shall like to answer a thousand questions." Happiness allowed her to write long letters but not much verse. She was astonished that "being too happy doesn't agree with literary activity."

Sometimes they quarrelled, often because she didn't eat enough. The worst non-dietary quarrel to date was over the identity of the Man in the Iron Mask. Robert "waxed hot" and

was still checking the identity thirty-six years later when he un-productively interrogated Don Carlos, pretender to the thrones of Spain and France. As a last resource, Robert always had a trump to play. "Now, Ba," he would say, "wouldn't it have been wrong if we two had not married?" She had to admit that she had been obstinately wrong in having demurred when he proposed. He would attempt to persuade her to, or dissuade her from, an action, but in the end he insisted that she have her way. To please him, she acquiesced.

Monday, November 15, was the feast day of St. Leopold and the name-day of the Grand Duke. Glittering marquises and dukes fortified with champagne acted as sentinels at the palace. Leopold II and his duchess appeared, the people shouted, the band played, a hymn was sung, and the Brownings hung draper-ies of crimson silk out their front windows. Their apartment in the piazza allowed Elizabeth to sit with her feet on her own fender and return the nods of their royal highnesses. She was filled with "throbs and thrills."

In their building was a cook who gave them English mutton chops at "Florentine prices." At their second Christmas dinner together they ate "plum puddingo" and Wilson's kneadcakes. Friend Father Prout passed through Florence and kissed Robert on the street. (Father Prout was the pen name of F. S. Mahony, an Irish humorist and correspondent at Rome to the *Daily News* of London.) Robert would go to Vieussseux' library (for men only), read the newspapers, and bring home news to Elizabeth. She waxed "fat and rosy."

After more than a year in Italy, Wilson was becoming Italian-ate enough to speak some of the language "with a little license in the grammar." She and Mrs. Loftus's maid had tickets to a reception at the Grand Ducal court, where they took an unob-trusive position near the door of one of the reception rooms. She was loyal enough to observe that the court was "shabby" in comparison with the English court. (Had Wilson been received at Buckingham Palace?) Her native Yorkshire had not condi-tioned her to look at nudes. Stopped dead in her tracks at the door of the Tribune in the Uffizi, she was unable to take one step within because of the "indecency" of the *Medici Venus* and of Titian's *Venus of Urbino* "painted stark, just overhead." Elizabeth thought that the "troublesome modesty" might subside if Wilson tried again. Robert thought that a "hysterical affection" followed by "presentiments" took possession of "her poor foolish brain" whenever she looked steadily at pictures.

The year 1848 was a year of thwarted revolution on the Continent. There was a *festa* to celebrate the granting of a constitution in Tuscany, and the Brownings again had thrilling sights. Elizabeth was undressing for bed when Robert called her to the window, whence they saw the torchlight parade and illuminated buildings, and heard the cheering. They indicated their liberal approval by putting two wax candles in each of their windows.

In March Elizabeth suffered her second miscarriage. This time they had known she was pregnant and were assembling baby things, some of which came from her sisters in England. Therefore, the disappointment was greater, and Elizabeth could not bear to look at the little clothes in the drawer. Always the thought lurked that the morphine was to blame, but Dr. Harding said no. Indeed he advised against too sudden a reduction in the dosage. He blamed the port wine that Dr. Cook had prescribed and that Robert had pressed on his wife. Robert blamed the "too long letters" she *would* write the day before the miscarriage. Again, her recovery was remarkable.

Dr. Harding recommended fresh air, and Robert engaged a carriage for a month, a *britska* with two horses and a coachman. By early April she had been out seven times in the carriage, and she was not tired by daily two-hour drives about the city and through the Cascine.

Perhaps one circumstance that influenced the Brownings' decision to stay in Florence that summer was that the vulgar English were also cowardly and were fleeing the revolutionary turbulence. Elizabeth observed that "the majors and gallant captains were the first to go." "Unless there's a general," she added.

Casa Guidi
May 9, 1848 to June 30, 1849

In April their six-months' lease of the flat on the square came to an end, and plans had to be made. They came to the conclusion that they had been "throwing money into the Arno" by taking furnished rooms. They could rent unfurnished rooms at much less and purchase their own furniture for almost nothing. Robert looked about. The suite in Casa Guidi that they had occupied in the fall was available unfurnished for twenty-five guineas a year. Six rooms – "three of them quite palace rooms" – plus two terraces and a kitchen. Furthermore, when they were away, as they quite often would be, they could sublet for ten pounds a month, and the subrental money would actually contribute towards their travelling expenses to England. They signed a year's lease and soon acquired enough furniture to let them take occupancy on May 9, 1848.

Furnishing a Fitting Habitation

It is remarkable how soon the Brownings were able to furnish their rooms. The Guidi furniture had been "fit for entertainment for the court of Tuscany," and Robert would seem to want to equal it. He was "far more particular" than Elizabeth about "horses, furniture, houses and carriages." "*A bas les aristocrats!*" she would cry whenever he was too particular. He also had more of a flair for decorating. After he signed the lease, surely he spent his days combing Florence and environs for the essentials. They planned to spend their last two winters' royalties of fifty pounds on the furniture, but, like newlyweds before and since, they spent more, even though Florence in 1848 was "the cheapest moment in the cheapest place." When they moved in, they had already spent ten pounds more than their budgeted fifty.

One may imagine the fluttering pulses of the Florentine merchants when word got round that "English millionaires," as the poets were thought to be, were furnishing an apartment in Casa Guidi. The merchants were to learn that Robert drove a hard bargain. The Brownings were not millionaires, though they lived well. Their first year in Italy had cost them less than £300 including Dr. Cook's bills for Elizabeth and Wilson, who was herself an "expensive maid" at £16 a year. For what they spent, Elizabeth said, "one may live much like the Grand Duchess," who lived in the Pitti Palace. To their charwoman, whose wage was six shillings a month, the difference between three hundred a year and three million was not obtrusively apparent. If the charwoman had but the good sense to save her wages for thirty-three months, she would have the £10 that the Brownings spent on material for their curtains.

They slept first in a borrowed bed, because Robert wanted "a ducal bed" for them – "all gilding and carving" and was willing to wait a bit for what he wanted. They bought (£1.10s) the framework for the great bed from Count Cottrell and ordered from a a manufactory a mattress with springs and down pillows (above £6) and later white muslin bed curtains. From the first, Wilson had her own iron bedstead, curtains and all. Iron or brass bedsteads were necessities in Florence, "because wood is a harbour for things unclean," the very thought of which made Elizabeth uncomfortable.

She teased Robert for coveting chests-of-drawers, and he reproached her for her "sofa plague." When they counted, they found that Robert had only six chests, whereas Elizabeth had eight sofas: three spring sofas in the drawing room, one in the little sitting room, a large one in the bedroom, and three others sprinkled "here and there." Two weeks after the inventory, Elizabeth mentions two new, unstuffed sofas with "skeleton arms" awaiting springs and covering of crimson satin, Robert having earlier bought some second-hand crimson satin from "cardinals' beds."

Their first chest-of-drawers, walnut inlaid with ivory, had belonged to the Guidi and had originally stood in the bedroom, where it remained. Then Robert bought (£2) a companion chest, ebony and ivory inlaid, with gilt handles of Tritons holding masks. Other chests followed.

Elizabeth suspected that she enjoyed the armchairs most, particularly hers, which was "very low," and "very languid look-ing." "You sink into it as into a nest of air," she said, and find "difficulty in getting up." On the night of October 8, 1848, it proved treacherous. "Bewitched by a spirit of foolishness," she knelt down in it to say her prayers, and the chair tipped forward, throwing her "head foremost" on the carpeted floor. Thereafter she prayed in the "common chair" she had been in the habit of using.

From Baron de Poillet, the French Chargé d'Affaires, who was leaving Florence and only awaiting his replacement, they bought the best of their furniture: a beautiful mirror, a sofa, a *secrétaire*, armchairs, and other things. His bed, which they declined to buy, must have been too expensive or less ducal than baronial. They hung the mirror above the fireplace in the draw-ing room. Its gilt frame with two carved cupids supporting can-dle holders was the most beautiful frame Elizabeth had seen in her life.

One of Robert's best finds was a large wood bookcase with brass diamond panelled screen and carved angels, serpents, and infants. It had come from a convent. Willing to risk being an occasion of horror to the carved angels, they talked of buying the novels of Balzac "in full" some day and shelving them in the bookcase. In the meantime they sent home for their own books. Against the opposite wall they placed another, open bookcase of carved wood.

In December Robert bought a third bed "at singular cheap-ness" (£6). In time of Elizabeth's illness he would require a proper bed for himself instead of one of the many sofas. The pur-chase included mattresses, pillows, quilt, two blankets, muslin curtains, and gilt ornaments for the top of the bed and the bed-posts. Except for her down pillows, Elizabeth preferred the new bed to their own. Everybody said it was a "wonderful bargain." It must have been set up in the back room that Robert was then using as a dressing room.

Other purchases arrived. For the drawing room a carpet (£8) and a second-hand Venetian glass chandelier (£2). For the din-ing room a sideboard, six teaspoons, and two tablespoons. They never acquired much plate, but then they did not entertain. Delivery men came with rococo chairs, marble-topped tables, washstands, and a huge oil jar for catching rain water. From a convent in Urbino came the sideboard and a seat of carved wood (both for £4). The sideboard was one hundred years old with carved "figures at the sides, old men's heads for handles & locks of gilt bronze." The seat, which they put in the drawing room, was carved, "all in grinning heads & arabesques," and enlivened by the poets with a crimson velvet cushion and crimson velvet for the back.

All was arranged in the "graceful disorder" Elizabeth loved in a room.

In November they were making the "greatest fuss" about the curtains and had not yet installed bellpulls to summon Wilson. From the merchant son of their "obliging" banker they ordered untold yards of English white mull muslin, enough to curtain the ten enormous windows and the ducal bed. The new, imported muslin *was* expensive (£10). The tops of all the windows were of "crimson imitation of damask" bought from Baron de Poillet. Each dining-room window had also a red curtain crossed with another of white muslin. (Elizabeth made a little sketch to help her sister visualize.) For the drawing-room windows they used their cardinals' crimson satin with yellow flowers, the crimson curtains crossed by white muslin. The curtains in the bedrooms were all of white muslin with the crimson damask window tops. By mid-December the curtains were up and the chimney pieces in the drawing and dining rooms covered with crimson velvet, as people did on the Continent. All agreed with Elizabeth that the rooms looked beautiful. "I love this house," she said.

In January came tables, books, crimson cushion, inkstand, wall clock, butter-stand, and other possessions of Elizabeth's that had been stored in London. Robert himself unpacked the great box, taking from the packing flannel, cambric, and cotton balls a portrait of Elizabeth's father, who never forgave his daughter's marriage. The picture was to be hung in the bedroom opposite the bed, though Elizabeth said, "I tremble to look at the dear face again."

In January 1850 Elizabeth mentions that they had bought three great pieces of tapestry, which they hung in the drawing and dining rooms. One of these, a large oblong tapestry (almost six feet high and seventeen feet wide) showed Hermes driving the cattle of Apollo and Apollo piping among his herds. The horse in this panel inspired the horse imagery in Robert's "Childe Roland to the Dark Tower Came."

> I never saw a brute I hated so –
> He must be wicked to deserve such pain.

A companion panel represented Maia showing the infant Hermes to Zeus, and Apollo piping to mortals. (These two panels brought £1,400 at auction in 1913 and may be seen today in the dining room of Vizcaya, the Miami mansion of the late James Deering.)

Robert was also buying pictures. In the early winter of 1849, he bought two wood panels of angels, and in the following May found some interesting things in a corn shop a mile outside Florence. He came home, described them to Elizabeth and persuaded her that they should buy them. When they arrived, the collectors were delighted to discover that the picture of "The Eternal Father" belonged with the angel side-panels. They reunited the three pieces and found that they had a Ghirlandaio altar piece, which they hung above the mirror in the drawing room.

Collecting was great fun. There was a *Crucifixion* that was "Giottesque" if not a Giotto; a Giottino "rarer than a Giotto"; a Pollaiuolo(?) *Christ at the Column*. Seymour Kirkup, an artist and necromancer whose house was on the Ponte Vecchio, used magic names: Giotto, Cimabue, Gaddi. Never mind that today's experts disagree with these attributions. The poets were pleased, and some of the paintings appear in the poem "Old Pictures in Florence," in which Robert blames Austrian rule for the Italians' neglect of their old masters.

While Robert was out searching for bargains, Elizabeth remained at home reading all the new books she could get, although the Vieusseux Library seemed to have taken "a vow against new books." When straits were dire, she re-read old favorites.

During this summer of 1848, their second in Florence, Robert was able to persuade her to do as the Florentines did to keep out the heat. The first summer, she had required, against his advice, that only the exterior blinds be closed during the day. Then she learned that with the protection of closed blinds, windows, and interior shutters, the thermometer indoors registered 71 degrees when the thermometer outdoors read 80 degrees. (When the thermometer in England is in the 70's, some people are laid low. Italian heat is different. To this day, the women of Florence who provide hospitality in their excellent pensions find it difficult to convince Anglo-Saxons that the Florentine way is best.) At sunset, the windows, closed in the morning, were opened to admit the cool air, and the terrace was sprinkled with cold water.

Evenings after tea they took walks, leaving the house at eight o'clock and remaining out till past nine. The streets that summer were "tolerably clean of the English," Elizabeth said. Often she and Robert walked at her pace down the Via Guicciardini, across the Ponte Vecchio, to the square, where they sat in the Loggia and admired Cellini's bronze *Perseus*. Just as often they walked the length of the Via Maggio to the Santa Trinita bridge, where they sat and watched the "divine sunsets." She preferred the sunsets to the *Perseus*. Nature she loved and next to nature art.

Robert was much less troubled that summer by the frequent headaches that often plagued him. These headaches may have been caused by his distinctive eyesight: his right eye was near-sighted and his left, far. "He used for all purposes a single eye," wrote his friend Mrs. Orr. "The two did not combine in their action." With his telescopic left eye he could read the number of a picture at the "end of a long gallery," and he liked to demonstrate that with his microscopic right eye he could copy an ode of Horace on a piece of paper the "size of a three-penny bit." (By the same token, Robert's penchant for writing companion poems in which he presented two sides to the same question may be related to the fact that he looked at every object through a microscope or through a telescope but never in focus: he was physiologically obliged to take distinct or even disparate points of view of every object, be it up at a villa or down in the city.)

Un Bel Giro
July 17 to August [7?], 1848

During the last two weeks in July and the first week in August, the Brownings went on an excursion. On Monday, July 17, they entrusted Casa Guidi to the care of the porter and, with their necessities packed in only two carpet bags, took the diligence to Arezzo, travelling through the night "for coolness." After three days, they "fled" the heat of Fano, where they were too favorably impressed by Guercino's *Guardian Angel* in Saint Augustine's Church. At Ancona they lived for a week on fish and cold water, and Robert wrote a poem inspired by the *Guardian Angel*:

> We were at Fano, and three times we went
>   To sit and see him in his chapel there,
> And drink his beauty to our soul's content
>   – My angel with me too:
> * * *
> Dear and great Angel, wouldst thou only leave
>   That child, when thou hast done with him, for me!

"Demoralized" out of "decency" by the heat, Elizabeth reclined on a sofa in petticoat and wrapper with her hair "dishevelled at full length." They approved of the mosaics and pine forest at Ravenna, but the marshes "sent up stenches" and the canal "exhalations." Elizabeth was "quite furious" at being denied admission to Dante's tomb without "special permission," and both were too angry to think of applying to the authorities. Instead, they peered through a grated window at Dante's epitaph inside. Between three and four in the morning, they stood outside the mausoleum and then took the carriage straight back to Florence, which was "as cool as an oven after the fire."

★

Not long after the excursion, Robert was laid up for a month with fever and ulcerated sore throat. He refused to see a doctor, and his "burning hands and languid eyes" frightened Elizabeth into "a paroxysm." At this critical moment Father Prout appeared unheralded at the door of Casa Guidi. He took charge, as he was equipped to do because he was a Jesuit, and Jesuits were "learned in all arts." He handled Elizabeth by jesting at her fright and handled Robert by forcing him to drink a concoction of port wine beaten up with the yolks of two eggs. At once Robert slept, and the fever subsided. Elizabeth was grateful to the "clever," "accomplished," "warm-hearted" Irishman. She had not imagined that there could exist such brilliancy in conversation. She was obliged to say, however, that he displayed a certain lack of "delicacy": he smoked cigars and used one of her "Raffael-basins" as "an instrument for spitting." Then, as Dissenter to Dissenter, she whispered to Arabel that Father Prout was "perhaps a Christian man in the large sense."

Alessandro cried, "*O Inglesi!*" when he saw the potion of eggs and port. The Brownings had engaged their first man servant. He did the marketing and cooking, proving a "master" at beefsteak pies and fricassees, and an "artist" at bread puddings and apple dumplings. How pleased with himself he looked the day he roasted and placed on the dining-room table a splendid turkey that had cost one shilling and ten pence in the market. Alessandro ruled the kitchen as his demesne and was not prone to brook interference from Wilson, who was prone to interfere. He had spent a month in London and could give as good as he got when Wilson harped on how much better everything was back home. (Elizabeth was disdainful of "boastful Britons.") With reason he complained about the size of the kitchen and the ladder to the kitchen loft. To him it was "extraordinary" to see a man sitting by his wife all day, as Robert sat beside Elizabeth!

Il Promesso Sposo

Although Wilson had to retire from every battle with Alessandro in the kitchen, she was not distressed. She was engaged to be married. For some time she and a uniformed member of the Grand Duke's bodyguard had been aware of each other in the Piazza Pitti. One of them arranged an introduction through a friend since proper Victorian maids did not drop handkerchiefs. Signor Righi was tall, dark, handsome, amiable, and well disposed towards Englishwomen as wives, because they were good housekeepers and *faithful*! He was the son of a "medical man" in Prato, where his brother was a rich haberdasher, and where his mother said she approved of the match. Even Robert thought him "very good and superior." Wilson, who was too sensible to choose the tall guardsman "on the mere strength of his externals," waited six months after his avowal before they exchanged rings of betrothment. Her fluency in Italian improved remarkably.

Members of the ducal guard might not marry while in office, but Signor Righi could expect another post in the palace, because he was educated, wrote a good hand, and knew Latin. (It is unlikely that the Englishman who pressed Wilson to come home and marry him knew Latin.) Alas, when patriots asked the Grand Duke to leave Florence, he dissolved the palace staff, and Signor Righi returned to his mother in Prato. For a time, he and Wilson corresponded, but then his letters stopped coming. She was slow to realize that she had been jilted. Signor Righi was false! A few months later Elizabeth wrote that Wilson was "*over* it completely" and in excellent spirits. "How could she continue to love such a man?"

A Child at Casa Guidi

At four o'clock in the morning of Friday, March 9, 1849, Robert stopped pacing the floor and wrote to Henrietta Barrett that at a quarter past two Elizabeth had given birth to a baby boy. For twenty-one hours her tiny body had endured the birth pains without a cry or a tear. Robert sat by her side through the ordeal until finally he had to be sent away, leaving Dr. Harding, the nurse, and Wilson to minister to his wife. At last he heard a new, strong voice through the thick wall and double doors that separated the drawing room from the bedroom. It was well after nine o'clock in the morning before he was allowed to see Elizabeth, who would not look at her son until Robert came to put the baby into her arms. (She had been living with the dreadful fear that a child born of her pain-racked body might be misformed.) The boy was not a day old when Robert said he could give his life for him already.

During this pregnancy, Elizabeth had done the impossible. She had given up the morphine. Moreover, she had compelled herself to eat for two, much as she would prefer to eat almost nothing at all. Her previous miscarriages supplied the motivation. She wanted a child even more than Robert did, and she realized more than Robert did that she was forty-three. The experienced Italian nurse, Signora Biondi, thought the baby "so strong, so strong" and that he had been "well nourished." The *balia* (wet nurse) arrived, and Baby was soon "feeding like a hungry man."

Elizabeth and Wilson had been sewing in anticipation, and clothes had come from Elizabeth's sisters in London. With "surprising art & success," Wilson had sewn everything for the "prettiest" open-work wicket cradle: the lining of pink twilled muslin, the embroidered curtains of white muslin (remnants from the drawing-room curtains), the pink pillow covered with muslin and frilled, the little linen sheets with edging, and a Marseilles quilt.

Elizabeth could not nurse her child, and during the first few days *balias* came and went before the proper one was found – a "mighty woman," aged twenty-six, with a month-old child of her own and fat cheeks that overflowed her neck as she bent down. The poets supplied her uniform: a large straw hat with blue streamers, gowns trimmed with blue ribbon, white collars and aprons. A baby girl would have required pink trimmings. The *balia* complimented the baby by saying he was "not at all like an English child."

There never was such a child. He was a slight-boned little creature, but so fat, double-chinned, rosy-cheeked, wide-chested, and strong-lunged that Elizabeth was "almost skeptical" of his being her child. The nurse thought it "*un miracolo*" that this baby had come from Elizabeth's tiny body. Wilson thought he looked like the Barretts, and Elizabeth thought his mouth and chin "facsimiles" of Robert's.

Robert sent three tufts of baby hair to relatives in England. Every morning he would go to the nursery to watch the baby being bathed, and he would walk up and down the terrace with his son in his arms. Flush did not share the poets' enthusiasm. He fell into a "deep melancholy" and made no effort to conceal his jealousy of the new creature on the lap where he was supposed to be. (Flush had ever been incapable of duplicity: in Wimpole Street he had more than once snapped at the trousered leg of the noisy poet who was pre-empting Elizabeth's attention.)

On June 26 the boy was baptized without godparents in the French Evangelical Protestant Church, which was the chapel of the Prussian Legation. Elizabeth chose the name – Robert Wiedemann Barrett Browning. The father was touched by the choice of Wiedemann, the maiden name of his mother, who had died unexpectedly in London a week after her grandson was born in Florence. When Wiedeman (as Elizabeth spelled the name) began to talk and tried to pronounce his name, he said "Penini," which, later shortened to "Peni" and finally to "Pen," became his nickname. He was always known to friends as Pen Browning. Back in London, John Kenyon allowed the poets £100 a year to help with the additional expenses of their household.

The Foreign Colony

We do not know just how many foreigners were in Florence in the Brownings' day, but one later estimate says that there were thirty thousand English and Americans living in Florence and environs at the outbreak of World War I. Before their marriage, Robert had said to Elizabeth that there were "hordes" of English in Florence and that they were "vulgar" and "pushing."

These hordes may be sub-divided. Some, like the Trollopes, were permanent residents or "hard core fixtures." Others were "floating" and came for an extended stay. Add to these the "birds of passage," who came for a week or a month.

The poets arrived in Florence determined to avoid their compatriots. Few English names appear in their early letters from Italy: Mrs. Jameson, Miss Boyle, and Father Prout were Irish; Mr. Ware, Mr. Hillard, and Mr. Powers, American; Mlle. de Fauveau, French; and the David Ogilvys, who also lived in Casa Guidi, were Scottish. Count Cottrell, who sold them their bed, and Seymour Kirkup, who made false attributions, were indeed English.

There were, moreover, no Italians. Most of the merchants they dealt with had foreign names: Vieusseux' library, Mme. Brecker's bookshop, Goodban's printshop, Doney's café, Philipson's bank, St. Paul's jewelry shop. English physicians wrote out prescriptions that English chemists filled. In later years, women with Italian names appear in the correspondence, but they were foreign women who had married Italians. Such a woman was referred to as "*Madame*" rather than as "*Signora*" or "Mrs." Mme. Tassinari was the English wife of the Grand Duke's chamberlain. Mme. Romagnoli was the English wife of the Brownings' servant. Why were there no Italians?

In Pisa, the poets had wished to meet Italians in order to practice the language. Professor Ferucci, introduced by Mrs. Jameson, had appeared for a brief moment and then disappeared. In Siena, Enrico Nencioni had met the Brownings at the Storys' villa – once. In Rome, Massimo d'Azeglio called – once. Elizabeth wrote to Mrs. Jameson, "As to Italian society, one may as well take to longing for the evening star, for it seems quite inaccessible." One exception was Pasquale Villari, who was on the edge of the Brownings' circle and later married an English wife.

In the eighteenth century, the typical English on the grand tour were people of quality who arrived with letters to Italians of quality. In Romantic days, Shelley knew Italians, and nobody could have more intimate relations with Italians than Lord

Byron. Then middle-class English came with their manners and tastes and preference for the society of each other. It was not uncommon for them to arrive in Rome, confine themselves to the "English ghetto" near the Piazza di Spagna, play billiards, and depart without having visited the Vatican.

The Italian nobility did not feel deprived of the company of the touring or resident English. A typical Florentine count might have two hundred cousins among the Medici, Ridolfi, Guidi, Rucellai, and other noble families. Through their agents, they were prepared to rent living space to the foreigners, but they preferred the society and manners of their own cousins. During their years of married life in Italy, Robert and Elizabeth never broke bread with the Medici, or Ridolfi, or Guidi, or Rucellai.

Florentines called their city The City of Flowers. The French said it was "*une ville toute anglaise.*" The English called it "a sunny place for shady people." Who were these people? Why did they come? How did they live? The principal attraction of Florence was that it supplied a haven for "impecunious English people." Of course, the churches and galleries were worth visiting by foreigners so inclined, but culture was less of a drawing card than the price of lodgings, food, wine, carriages, and servants. The Brownings' "Dearest Isa" Blagden lived in a fourteen-room villa on Bellosguardo. She had a man servant, a maid servant, and a carriage. She held open house every Saturday. Because she was poor, she had to share expenses with a paying guest. Her share amounted to £10 a month. *14*

There were almost no police, for there was almost no crime. People were not mugged, nor were cocker spaniels kidnapped on the streets of Florence. Flush could go out by himself and return unharmed. Elizabeth liked to disparage England and let pass no opportunity to point out that in Italy people of all classes walked in the same gardens, looked at the same pictures, heard the same operas, and mingled in the same crowds with gladness and harmony. She wondered why English crowds should vent themselves in outbursts of drunkenness, brutality, fisticuffs, and blasphemy despite their advantages of "scriptural instruction." Unlike Elizabeth, Robert and Wilson became more jingoistic and Anglophile the farther they went from home.

There were amenities additional to the "celestial cheapness." The Grand Duke would tip his hat to foreigners when their paths crossed. Vulgar pushers were "*signoria*'d and *eccellenza*'d" by servants, menials, and merchants, until the foreigners thought that they deserved the deference. Most English felt that they could patronize Italians. Isa Blagden was an angel, "universally beloved," probably illegitimate, and the author of a few dreadful novels. Pasquale Villari was a patriot, distinguished scholar, and historian. Yet Isa thought she was paying a compliment when she told him, "I have always said that you are the only Italian who can write an essay." Wilson looked down on Annunziata and on Italians in general.

Divertimenti

During the social season, a foreigner might attend as many balls, concerts, and receptions as anybody could possibly desire. There were weekly balls at the Pitti Palace, others at the foreign legations, and still others at the Casino dei Nobili. Almost every resident Englishwoman had her "day" at home. Any Friday, one could call on Mrs. Trollope, who was "vulgar"; any Saturday on Miss Blagden, who was the Brownings' dearest friend in Italy. Many of the thousand villas that surround and enhance Florence were rented for little and staffed for less. These villas supplied elegant settings for teas, receptions, concerts, and theatricals.

T. A. Trollope in *What I Remember* describes the Pitti Palace balls provided every Tuesday by the Grand Duke, who appeared at these receptions only once a year. At the first rout of the season, when court dress or uniform was required, Leopold II and his duchess walked through the palace rooms thronged with seven hundred guests. On subsequent Tuesdays the seven hundred fared without the Duke and without court dress. The lack of exclusiveness staggered one English nobleman who reported in audience that his London tailor had been received in the same rooms as himself. "*Qu'importe?*" asked Leopold. The tailor spent in Florence money he had earned in London, and

Leopold's duty was not to the enforcement of class distinctions but to the prosperity of his liege subjects, who had apartments to let and merchandise to sell. Wilson went and was not impressed.

The guests of the hospitable Hapsburgs "behaved abominably," we are told. When the "handsome and abundant" supper was spread, the English (but not the Americans) would empty plates of bonbons into their reticules. Some pushing people stuffed their pockets with large portions of ham, fowl, and/or fish, the fish first wrapped in newspaper brought along as a precaution to protect the pockets from the stains of *sauce mayonnaise collée*. On occasion, a shameless Continental countess might be observed at the buffet table carefully wrapping jelly in her lace *mouchoir*. After supper, the guests returned full-pocketed to the quadrilles. "The worst drawing room in Europe," sighed Leopold.

Other diversions included picnics, excursions, music, dancing, theater, amateur theatricals, opera, spiritualistic séances, whist, gambling, sex, and gossip. The picnics might extend for two or three days in such favorite places as Vallombrosa, Camaldoli, and especially Pratolino, a grand-ducal park seven miles from Florence. Music was inexpensive. Frederick Tennyson, elder brother of the laureate, was not rich, but he could engage an orchestra to play for him alone at breakfast and at musicales for his guests, the Brownings often included. Admission to the Pergola, the principal theater, cost one and a half pence. Having paid this sum, one might be wined and dined by friends who had boxes, which were more like drawing rooms to receive guests. Most of the time, people did not listen to the opera but chatted, ate, and drank quite sociably. The Brownings sometimes rented a box and served champagne.

Not Angels, but Angles

The fire of sex produced the smoke of gossip. "Scandal holds here its festival," wrote the biographer of Charles Lever. "Scandalous tongues . . . wag there incessantly," wrote W. R. Cassells. To him Florence was the "most scandalous and depraved town . . . in the world." Robert and Elizabeth loved the gossip and abundantly contributed to the smoke. She observed that English people came together to gamble or dance and departed for other activities best hinted at. Sometimes a husband had reason to suspect that the documented paternity of his wife's child was a false attribution. Sometimes a wife would run away with her Italian lover. In his late sixties, when Seymour Kirkup had "a long gray beard and glittering eye," he impregnated his servant, Regina Ronti, a maid in her teens. Robert took the view that the natural father was Regina's unidentified Italian lover, but Kirkup had reason to believe her attribution. Elizabeth kept on gossiping to the end, and Robert continued through the years he survived.

All gossip was heterosexual. Immune from hint of misdoing were the "emancipated women" who came to worship at the shrine of the woman whom Walter Savage Landor termed the "most magnificent English poet since Milton." Some of these emancipated ones "dressed like men down to the waist"; some contracted "female marriage" with each other; some exchanged wedding rings. Miss Haworth called while on "the honeymoon of her matrimonial alliance" with Miss Heaton. Miss Heaton, whom Elizabeth termed "*monsieur le Mari*," had "many excellent qualities," although "he" talked too much and "seldom ceased moving." Miss Cushman and Miss Hays called. They lived together, dressed alike, and had taken "vows of celibacy & eternal attachment to each other." Miss Cushman, who was an actress, had played Romeo one night and Juliet the next. "Though an actress," Elizabeth wrote, "Miss Cushman has an unimpeachable character. . . ." It was high praise to say that she was "manly" without being "masculine." There were many others – sculptresses, painters, actresses, or just independent spinsters. They adored Elizabeth, who had proved to the world that Woman (albeit happily married) could surpass Man, including her own husband, in creative achievement. Kate Field, a captivating young American, tells us how she entered the darkened drawing room at Casa Guidi, fell on her knees, and kissed Elizabeth's feet. In our day Virginia Woolf thought it fatal for a person to be man-manly or woman-

womanly. Elizabeth was a precursor of such advocacy of uni-
sex: she much admired the masculine women about her and felt
conversely compelled to say, "I hate and detest a masculine
man." No son of hers would grow up to be one.

In the summer, there was a general exodus of the Italians to
the sea coast and of the English to the Baths of Lucca. The Baths
consisted of three settlements, the first being *Ponte a Serraglio*
(410 feet in the mountains) about sixteen miles from the city of
Lucca. At *Ponte* were the assembly or ball rooms, the reading
room, the principal baths, and the gambling and billiard rooms,
for *Ponte* attracted pleasure lovers. "A sort of wasps' nest of
scandal and gaming," said Elizabeth.

A mile further were the *Bagni alla Villa* (490 feet), so called
because the villa of the Duke of Lucca was there. Here was not
frivolity but a Protestant English chapel, built largely through
the efforts of Mrs. Clotilda Stisted, "Queen of the Baths," who
graced *la Villa* with her residence and her eccentricities. To
help pay for the erection of the chapel, she wrote and sold *Letters from the Bye-Ways of Italy* (1845) in which she expressed
the wish that "our gracious Queen" would refuse passports to
certain types who were disgracing themselves at *Ponte* and
"particularly in Florence" and giving England a bad name. The
Brownings stayed at *Bagni alla Villa* during their second and
third visits to the Baths.

Less than a mile further were the mud baths of *Bagni Caldi*,
where the Brownings spent their first holiday at the Baths (1849)
in quiet seclusion from the merrymaking.

During their first years in Italy, the poets kept out of the swing.
As Elizabeth grew stronger, she was willing to receive guests: a
few permanent residents, some floaters, and many birds of passage, who came with letters of introduction. Robert became
willing to go out night after night, generally but not always without her. She became less of a recluse. Together they went to musicales, to the theater and opera, and even to a masked ball during carnival. On Sundays they attended the Swiss Evangelical
Church, where Dissenters worshipped. Wilson was loyal to the
Church of England establishment in Florence, where sixteen

pence admission was exacted at the door. (For that matter, a fee was required in those days for admission to Westminster Abbey.)

Casa Guidi provided a cultural oasis in the desert of "very un-intellectual" Anglo-Florence. Most of the people who called on the poets were "creative," and many of them were Americans. Elizabeth did not work hard at being a hostess, at the give and take of conversation. More than one visitor wrote that she sat in an armchair or lay on a sofa and neither laughed, smiled, nor spoke. Enrico Nencioni was disappointed that the little she said was said in English. We benefit, however, for, although shy in company, she talked, smiled, and laughed by post, and we have her correspondence.

Robert was the reverse. He was ebullient, quick-moving, "in-exhaustible," "infinitely talkative," and even in London could dominate a dinner party of ten or of forty. Always in the right, he could shout and stamp with rage to prove his point. Even when not aroused, his voice was loud and once was heard a half a mile from Isa Blagden's villa, where he was on the terrace de-nouncing something. The women adored him "far too much for decency," Elizabeth knew. "There was always a ripple of laugh-ter round the sofa where he used to seat himself," wrote Fran-ces Power Cobbe, "generally beside some lady of the company, towards whom, in his eagerness, he would push nearer and nearer till she frequently rose to avoid falling off at the end!" The men feared him, said T. A. Trollope, lest his "quiet, lurking smile" expose the shallowness of their utterances.

Bagni di Lucca
June 30 to October 17, 1849

For their third summer holiday in Italy, the Brownings decided to do as their compatriots did and to go to the Baths of Lucca, not to be sure to *Ponte*, where the giddy English went, but to the *Bagni Caldi*, a mountain village that provided silence and loneli-ness and coolness beside the stream among the rocks and chest-nut trees. They first went alone on an exploratory journey to the seashore, but high prices at the coast sent them to the mountains where for three months they rented "an eagle's nest" high above the "wasps' nest" of dissipation at *Ponte*. Then they returned to Florence to fetch Pen, Wilson, Alessandro, the *balia*, and Flush. They arrived back at the Baths on the evening of June 30.

Despite the pregnancies, the miscarriages, and the birth of her child, Elizabeth was stronger and able to do more than she had been capable of since she "arrived at woman's estate." The Cottrells and Ogilvys were at the Baths, and Elizabeth gave an "entertainment," at which she served Wilson's kneadcakes, Alessandro's breadcake, pigeon pie, ham, ricotta, figs, and strawberries. One day the Brownings made an excursion to the top of *Monte Prato Fiorito* (4,260 feet). They left at eight-thirty in the morning – Elizabeth, Wilson, and the *balia* on donkeys for much of the trip; Robert, Alessandro, and three guides on mountain ponies. They did not return until six in the evening.

Flush loved the hot, wet baths and was circumspect enough to have made, or pretend to have made, his peace with Baby. When he was required to function as pony with Wiedeman on his back, he turned his head round to kiss the bare dimpled feet. Wiedeman continued to achieve: he cut his first tooth. Sophia Cottrell's child was a year old but "nothing like the size" of Wiedeman at four months. At five months and three days he was brought in from the wings with a rose in each fist for Elizabeth and for Robert, who were observing their third wedding anniversary. (Props and choreography were by Wilson.) To match the roses in his cheeks, he wore rose ribbons in his cap and rose-colored knitted shoes. Robert fussed with Elizabeth for speaking to Baby in Italian. "I don't want him to be an Italian," Robert said; but Alessandro, the *balia*, and Wilson talked to him in Italian, and two languages would only confuse a six-month-old baby.

How Do I Love Thee?

After three years of marriage Elizabeth told her sister, "There is more love between us two at this moment, than there ever has been." One morning as Robert was standing at the window of their house in the mountains, she came to him and said, "Do you know I once wrote some poems about *you*? There they are, if you care to see them." He read through the forty-four sonnets and, tremendously moved, insisted that they be included in her next volume. In order to conceal the intensely personal nature of the verse, they chose a "purposely ambiguous" title: *Sonnets from the Portuguese*. The best known of these is number forty-three, which begins "How do I love thee? Let me count the ways." The next, and last, was written in the house on Wimpole Street two days before her marriage.

> Belovèd, thou hast brought me many flowers
> Plucked in the garden, all the summer through
> And winter, and it seemed as if they grew
> In this close room, nor missed the sun and showers.
> So, in the like name of that love of ours,
> Take back these thoughts which here unfolded too,
> And which on warm and cold days I withdrew
> From my heart's ground. Indeed, those beds and bowers
> Be overgrown with bitter weeds and rue,
> And wait thy weeding; yet here's eglantine,
> Here's ivy! – take them, as I used to do
> Thy flowers, and keep them where they shall not pine.
> Instruct thine eyes to keep their colors true,
> And tell thy soul their roots are left in mine.

> *Casa Guidi*
> *October 17, 1849 to August 31, 1850*

In the autumn they returned to Florence, very glad to get back to their own chairs and tables. They continued to lead a secluded life, although occasionally a visitor passing through Florence would call with a letter of introduction.

One of these was Margaret Fuller, who spent many evenings with the poets during that winter and spring. There was every reason for Elizabeth to love her: she was a militant feminist, an articulate liberal, and the intellectual equal of male Transcendentalists in Boston. No matter that she was somewhat angular and very plain and spoke French with a Boston accent. Before coming to Florence from Rome, she had astonished her friends by revealing that she had wed the Marquis Angelo Ossoli, who was handsome, penniless, and ten years her junior. Their son, Angelino, was a year old before his mother told her friends that he existed. At Casa Guidi she talked and the Marquis listened, rather the reverse of Robert and Elizabeth.

In December Elizabeth wrote home that she was expecting another child in April. She would love to have had a daughter, but she lost this child too. All her life she would "hanker after little girls."

Wiedeman continued to be unique in the history of mankind. On Christmas Day, when he was only nine months old, he crawled for the first time, and the poets threw things across the floor for Baby to pursue. At eleven months, he would laugh like an imp when he tipped over water jugs or pulled a broom to pieces. He convinced Elizabeth that he would grow up sensitive to poetry because, although he had not yet uttered a word, he liked anything rhythmical, and when he heard music, he would beat his face and head with his fists, break into ecstacies of laughter, and cause his father to say, "Ba, I do hope that child is not going mad." Robert and Elizabeth went to the shops themselves to buy his toys, and Papa spent a whole Sunday morning between breakfast and church in learning how to spin a top. The cap on Baby's golden fleece of curls was decked with feathers just like the caps of the little Italian princes.

In April, Robert published *Christmas Eve and Easter Day*, his first volume since his marriage. "Christmas Eve" examines three aspects of religious thought in mid-century: the simple in a Dissenting English chapel; the ritualistic in St. Peter's Basilica at midnight; and the rational in a lecture on the higher criticism by a hawk-nosed professor in the university at Göttingen. After honest examination of these three sides to the question that most troubled English Protestantism in his day, the poet prefers his own simple Dissent:

> My heart does best to receive in meekness
> This mode of worship, as most to His mind,

> Where earthly aids being cast behind,
> His All in All appears serene,
> With the thinnest human veil between.

In June, the *Athenaeum* magazine nominated Elizabeth to suc-
ceed Wordsworth in the laureateship, asserting in print that "no
living poet of either sex . . . can prefer a higher claim than Mrs.
Elizabeth Barrett Browning."

Villa Hunting
July 2, 1850

Early in July Robert spent a harrowing day in Siena, the first
time husband and wife had been separated for more than three
hours. They were perplexed as to where to spend the summer
months, and Robert was looking for a villa to rent. He left Florence at seven in the morning, minded to return by train at seven
in the evening, but there was no train "in consequence of a
festa," the famous Siena *Palio*. Elizabeth sat up until midnight
feeling as if she had lost her head. At three in the morning she
heard him calling to her softly in the Via Mazzetta beneath the
bedroom window. "Ba!" he called. "Robert!" she said, "is it
really you?"

Without waiting to put on slippers, she ran barefoot to the
nursery, awakened Wilson and the *balia*, who went down and
awakened the porter, who opened the street door for Robert. He
had travelled from Siena with two priests in a "halting crazy
vehicle," afraid lest Elizabeth be uneasy. Elizabeth felt guilty
that she had eaten an "excellent dinner" without him, whereas
he had taken only a glass of milk and some biscuits. In almost
four years of married life he had neither dined nor slept away
from his wife.

A cool villa for the summer was especially desirable because
Elizabeth was again pregnant. For six weeks she did not leave
Casa Guidi and took every precaution, spending her days on the
sofa; but on the morning of July 28 she had her fourth, last, and
most serious miscarriage. Dr. Harding had Elizabeth packed.in
ice for two days and told Robert that she had lost "above a

hundred ounces of blood" within twenty-four hours and that "not one in five thousand women" would have survived. All night Robert sat by the "little patient white face." She rallied – but slowly. In the third week after the miscarriage she could sit up every day but could not stand without help. The doctor advised a change of air in the country and discontinuance of all medicine.

Siena
August 31 to October [8?], 1850

At seven in the morning of August 31 they left by rail for Siena. Baby was in ecstasies in the train except when he discovered that his little arm could not reach the electric telegraph. (Baby could not grasp the telegraph wires for which he reached, but "a man's reach should exceed his grasp," as Father said in his next volume. "Or what's a heaven for?" he added.) They spent the night at a hotel, and the next day, Sunday, Robert found a small seven-room house with a garden about two miles from the city. The house was on *Poggio dei Venti*, deservedly named "Hill of the Winds." Baby took delight in the donkey, the pig, the pigeons, and the great yellow dog; but, he said (Elizabeth said), that he preferred the Austrian band in Florence. "We have just weaned him victoriously and finally," his mother wrote on September 21, her victory achieved with the help of aloes put on the *balia*'s breast. She was sent back to her own child, leaving Elizabeth's fat boy with "rose-coloured cheeks and a gigantic appetite." After eighteen months of breast feeding, he missed the *balia*.

Dr. Harding had been right about the country air. Before the month on the Hill of the Winds was out, Elizabeth felt as well as ever and could walk as much as a mile in the "English" lanes. *En route* back to Florence, they stayed a week or so in the hotel in Siena. Elizabeth, whom Robert had carried into the train a month previously, walked up the steps and through the Cathedral, through the churches, and through the galleries, where the pictures were "divine."

Casa Guidi
October 1850 to May 3, 1851

"The charm of a home is a home *to come back to*," Elizabeth wrote after they returned to their own books and spring sofas. Sitting together *en pantoufles* over coffee in the drawing room, one would say to the other, "Oh, how delightful this is! I do hope nobody will come tonight." Sometimes somebody came, and Robert had to remove his slippers for Goethe's grandson, or Charles Eliot Norton, or, of all people, Mrs. Trollope. It had taken Elizabeth forty months to wear down Robert's opposition to the woman who had in print disparaged the poetry of Victor Hugo. Mrs. T. was admitted in January and turned out to be "very agreeable, and kind, and good-natured." She granted the Brownings reciprocal admission to her "private days" (when she received *en ménage*). For them to attend her "heterogeneous" "public days" (*en ménagerie*) would have been unthinkable.

Elizabeth made it perfectly clear that her approval of Wiedeman was objective. "I don't love my child, now, only because he is my child . . . ," she wrote objectively to Henrietta, quoting Wilson's supportive opinion that "such a child, before, never was." Just about every day Robert measured Baby's height against the door, reporting "wonderful growth" – "some inch a week." (Pen was nineteen before Robert abandoned his ambition for a tall son.) Wiedeman and Flush became allies. When one of the poets had to scold a transgressing Flush, Baby would cry. When Baby was in a transgressing rage, Flush would lick Baby's arm and put instant stop to Baby's frenzied screams.

At a year and a half, Wiedeman couldn't, or wouldn't, speak a word. Like Flush, he employed gesture and symbol rather than language. His screams outside a church (of Rome) meant that he wanted to go within, kneel, turn up his eyes, and cross himself in worship. Pointing at his raised foot meant that Mama must pull off the little shoes and stockings, kiss the little feet, and go to the nursery while Wilson put Baby to bed. Then they would leave

Robert to himself in the drawing room. "Come back soon, Ba," he would say.

In the fifth year of their marriage, Elizabeth was at "the very height of her health." They took what Robert remembered as their longest walks – up the long "pull" to San Miniato and down the avenue of cypresses from *Poggio Imperiale*. But, as Robert wrote years later, they returned to England, "there was fatigue," and she "never touched that height again."

A "drop of gypsey blood" tingled in Elizabeth's veins as well as in Robert's. They loved to travel. In a carriage or train they were free of impediments and the possible delivery of a letter with bad news. The constant change of air did her good, and one could escape the "world and oneself" in the stack of novels they always carried with them. They did want to see Rome and Naples before they left Italy "for good," and they talked much of living in Paris, because it was nearer than Florence to London and their own dear relatives. Should they choose to settle in Paris, their furniture could be sent up the Rhone.

However, Robert was shrewd enough to try Paris before making the move. They decided to renew their lease on May 1 and to sublet their "old dear rooms" in Casa Guidi while they were away. At the end of their third year of occupancy, painters, cleaners, and upholsterers took over. Carpets came up, curtains came down, chairs were recovered, spring sofas renewed, and the nursery repainted. The apartment became "too perfect almost to leave!" To Robert, subletting proved "a good speculation," and he was able to say, "We gain decidedly," upon their return after eighteen months' absence, even though their renting agent proved less than adequate. Among their tenants was James Russell Lowell, who took the flat for two months in the fall of 1851.

En Route
May 3 to July 23, 1851

They left Florence on May 3, sharing a *vettura* with the Ogilvys. In Venice they were tourists – operas, gondolas, pigeons – for a month. When the Ogilvys went their own way, the travelers were not sad: there had been just too much conversation for Elizabeth's taste, and Mrs. Ogilvy had found it uncomfortable to travel in a carriage with "old mangy" Flush. The Brownings moved at their own pace through Milan, the Italian lakes, Switzerland, and Strasbourg, to Paris, where they arrived on June 30 and tarried for three weeks. Then they crossed the Channel and returned to England after an absence of five years. Elizabeth's first step on English ground was into a puddle.

London
July 23 to September 25, 1851

At the end of May, Elizabeth's publisher had brought out her *Casa Guidi Windows*, a slim volume with a title appropriate for a political poem by a woman who loved to look out windows. Through her, Wiedeman would teach Mankind to look to the future with hope.

> The sun strikes, through the windows, up the floor;
> Stand out on it, my own young Florentine,
>   Not two years old, and let me see thee more!
> It grows along thy amber curls, to shine
>   Brighter than elsewhere. Now, look straight before,
> And fix thy brave blue English eyes on mine,
>   And from thy soul, which fronts the future so,
> With unabashed and unabated gaze,
>   Teach me to hope for, what the angels know
> When they smile clear as thou dost.

The London world of stage and book lionized the returning poets. ("A strange thing . . . ," Miss Mitford said, "to see Miss Barrett walking about like other people.") Reunion with relatives was more important than being lions. With Baby, Elizabeth stole visits to her old house when Grandpapa Barrett was not at home. (She was compelled to observe that 50 Wimpole Street could do with a thorough cleaning.) They visited Robert's old house at New Cross, where Wiedeman made new conquests of Aunt Sarianna and Grandpapa Browning, who was "Nonno" to Baby. While his wife and son were stealing a visit in Wimpole Street, Robert visited St. Marylebone Church nearby, knelt, and kissed the paving stones in front of the door he had passed through to marry Elizabeth. Wilson spent a fortnight in Yorkshire, where her mother lived near Sheffield. During this fortnight, Elizabeth dressed herself and tended Baby, who was distraught without "Lily," as he called Wilson.

Much as Robert loved the activity of London, he was alarmed by the effect of English air on Elizabeth's health. In consequence of puddles and fog, she had begun to cough before they reached London, whereas in Italy she had had no such cough or difficulty in breathing. After Wilson returned from Yorkshire, Robert took his family to Paris. Elizabeth slept perfectly at Dieppe and soon her cough almost wholly vanished.

Paris
September 26, 1851 to July 5, 1852

During the eight-hour channel crossing, everybody, including Flush and Thomas Carlyle, was seasick. The Brownings rented an apartment in Paris and hired a housemaid-cook named Desirée. The apartment was large, well furnished, sunny, and, best of all, had windows and a terrace on the Champs Elysées. "Not for the Alps" would Elizabeth have missed on December 2 the sight of Louis Napoleon (who had that very day dissolved the French Assembly) riding beneath her windows amid music, shouting, white horses, and glittering helmets. On January 4, Robert abandoned his New Year's resolution to write a poem every day. In February they called on George Sand, Elizabeth noting in sorrow that the young men around her idol used tobacco and "ejected saliva."

In March Robert had to reprimand Elizabeth for leaving church (French Evangelical) before communion service was over. She stayed, though, to the very end of *La Dame aux Camélias* in which Fechter and Madame Doche were appearing. (Camille was an invalid with a racking cough who loved Armand, who had nothing to offer but his love. His father separated the lovers, and Camille died.) The "too exquisite" acting "almost killed" Elizabeth out of her "propriety." She "sobbed so" she could scarcely keep her place and had "a splitting headache" for twenty-four hours. Tears ran down Robert's cheeks, and Elizabeth was ill for two days. She could not bear to accept Mrs. Jameson's invitation to see the play a second time.

What a joy it was to shop in Paris! On the Place Vendôme, Elizabeth bought a drawn maroon satin bonnet trimmed with maroon velvet. It cost fifteen shillings, but Robert was "tolerably satisfied" with it. For Peni she found a black velvet frock to wear to a children's New Year's Eve party. Because her blue gown was singed, she bought a new gown of the finest merino extant, in the latest fashion – *à la Basquine*, because Louis Napoleon's Eugénie was a Basque.

In March Robert attended a series of Tuesday lectures on Elizabeth's poetry given by a French critic at the *Collège de France* and wept at the appreciation of his wife's verse, although Elizabeth was vexed by the "painful inaccuracies" of some of the biographical details.

A few cold days in December brought back Elizabeth's "tiresome" cough and took away her voice. In the spring, she again caught cold and coughed. Paris was not for them, as much as Robert liked the city. "I love Italy, and like Paris," she said. Their decision was to go to England that summer and then return to Italy for the winter. She bought two new summer dresses and another bonnet before they departed for London.

London
July 6 to October 12, 1852

Soon after they settled in London, Robert had to sleep away from his wife in order to establish his father in Paris. Grandpapa Browning, who was a widower of seventy, had lost a suit for breach of promise of marriage brought by Minny Von Müller, a twice-widowed neighbor of forty-five. Rather than pay £800 damages awarded by the court, Nonno chose to resign his clerkship in the Bank of England and to live on his pension with his daughter, Sarianna, in Paris. Elizabeth thought him "the poor victim of a villainous woman," and Lord Campbell, the presiding judge, praised the felicitous style of the fifty-odd love letters that "Dearest Minny" exhibited in evidence. There might have been an amicable settlement had not Robert, in eruption, written an injudicious letter to the widow, inspired his father to write her a libelous letter, and infuriated the plaintiff. In later years, Sarianna censored Robert's correspondence lest his "turbulence" stir up "newspaper warfare."

It has been suggested that during this brief first separation from his wife Robert wrote "In Three Days."

> So, I shall see her in three days
> And just one night, but nights are short,
> Then two long hours, and that is morn.
> See how I come, unchanged, unworn –
> Feel, where my life broke off from thine,
> How fresh the splinters keep and fine, –
> Only a touch and we combine!

To add to the vexation of the summer, Wilson mustered up the pluck to ask that her wages be raised from sixteen pounds to twenty guineas a year. (After all, she had received sixteen pounds as a lady's maid and nothing more when she became a nursemaid as well.) Even though the increase would amount to only two shillings a week, it was out of the question, and the request pained Elizabeth, who had thought that Wilson cared more for her and Baby than to leave them so. Happily, within the month Wilson had second thoughts and confessed that she could not bear separation from Penini or his mother, and that sixteen pounds a year would continue to suffice.

On October 12, the Brownings left London for Paris, where they stayed almost a fortnight before beginning the journey back to Casa Guidi.

Casa Guidi
November 1852 to July 15, 1853

Their "acres" of apartment space in Casa Guidi seemed better than ever after the furnished rooms they had rented in London. To Elizabeth, the still warm "old nest" looked exactly as if they had left it yesterday, and she enjoyed the "sound of our dear Italian." Robert was able to report that the profit made on subletting allowed them to live rent free for six months. They resumed their former "hermit life."

Robert rose at seven and went to the sitting room, where his dressing required more time than did Elizabeth's. She had to remain in bed until Wilson dressed herself, dressed Penini, and then came to the bedroom to bathe and dress her mistress. Promptly at nine breakfast was served by their new manservant. (Vincenzo was most regular, attentive, and rigorous in his duties, providing "not a hair breadth's excuse" for criticism; but, because he looked like a "subsidiary stableman" and exuded odors, they planned to let him go when they could find a good-looking replacement.) Between breakfast and dinner at three there was a long morning in which to work: Robert in the little sitting room at the escritoire writing *Men and Women*, Elizabeth in her armchair in the drawing room writing *Aurora Leigh*.

Evenings they spent at home during this happy winter with "nothing from without to vex" them much. Elizabeth sat in her armchair lost in a book borrowed from Mme. Brecker's library, as Robert sat beside her reading Vasari's *Lives of the Painters* for material to be converted next morning into dramatic monologues. Sometimes one poet read aloud to the other. When Wilson had to leave Penini to put Elizabeth to bed, Robert went to the nursery and sat by his son lest the boy awaken alone. If Penini did wake up, Robert sang him quietly back to sleep.

Some afternoons they paid "morning calls" and sometimes took a trip to Prato or Fiesole. Two or three times a week visitors came for tea or coffee, people like Frederick Tennyson, Hiram Powers, Robert Lytton, or an American in passage. Elizabeth, who had gone for years without owning a thimble, now helped make frocks for her son. Robert, who used to force her to drink chianti or port, now forced cod liver oil upon her.

Elizabeth was predisposed to mysticism and the occult and wanted intensely to believe in the spiritualism that raged through Europe and America in the 1850's. Straining to communicate with the living in a materialistic age, spirits rapped, tables tipped, invisible hands wrote, guitars played by themselves, humans levitated, furniture floated, and uneducated mediums spoke Greek. Believers experimented around a table in the drawing room at Casa Guidi, but to no avail. The believers thought that Robert, the only skeptic present, drove the spirits away. Husband and wife had contrasting attitudes towards mesmerism, too. "Humbug!" Robert said, when she arranged for a "magnetizer" to give a demonstration in her drawing room. As the man was attempting to magnetize Signorina Biondi, Elizabeth herself swooned away into a hypnotic trance. An unconvinced Robert insisted it was only "a common fainting fit."

"Robert won't let me take Penini with us when we pay a morning visit," Elizabeth told Henrietta, remarking that her boy (in his fourth year) was "just made to be carried about and shown off, with his long purple feather shaking over his trailing golden ringlets, and the small black silk jacket I have just finished embroidering for him." Whenever a visitor came to Casa Guidi, Penini was on stage "two minutes afterwards." Sometimes Robert played on the pianoforte and Peni danced with a tambourine, giving Father directions as to tempo. "Such steps, such attitudes," Mother said and avowed, "Certainly there never was such a darling since the world began." When she began teaching him to read, his attention span lasted "about five minutes." (When he was a young man at Oxford, his span at books was not much greater.)

One early summer day at two in the morning, a distracted Wilson awakened the poets with the news that Vincenzo was violently ill. Robert awakened the porter, who went for the doctor, who feared apoplexy, and bled the patient. The medical man thought that Vincenzo had been eating and drinking too much and advised that he leave the Brownings' service to recuperate. Vincenzo was as pleased with the separation as were the poets, who gave him his wages to the end of the month and a gift as well. Soon thereafter Elizabeth was beside herself when the news came that Vincenzo was in the hospital with miliary fever, which was characterized by a rash resembling measles and was "most infectious." Vincenzo's bedroom had been close to Penini's, so his mattresses were instantly carried out into the courtyard to be thoroughly washed. Penini was not infected.

Girolama

The only regular dinner guest who came to Casa Guidi during these months was a little Italian seamstress named Girolama. She was "head and shoulders" shorter than Elizabeth, who wrote home that they had Girolama in to dinner quite often "purely to please Pen," to whom she was "comrade and friend."

The story the little seamstress told some fifty years later presents Elizabeth in a different and most endearing light. Girolama lived in the Piazza Pitti with her father, who was groom to the Grand Duke, and her mother, who was a seamstress. She was an attractive girl with a body of medium size but with legs hardly more than a foot long. When she sat at her window, her dwarfish size was not apparent, and at eighteen she was courted by a fair-haired Austrian officer who had seen her only at the window. When he finally saw her standing, he was disillusioned and broke her heart.

Elizabeth heard this story and invited Girolama to Casa Guidi. Together the women sewed, while Girolama sat on a little stool beside the lady's armchair. The lady spoke "many kind words" and stroked the hair of the heart-broken girl. Elizabeth herself had been a young woman who had abandoned the hope of being loved. Then she had heard the step on the stair.

1 Casa Guidi about 1916. The Brownings' living rooms were on the first floor and
overlooked the Via Mazzetta, to the left.
The entrance to the building was on the Via
Maggio, to the right. *From a postcard
made for Mrs. Ellen Hutchinson Centaro.*

2 *above* The drawing room after restoration in 1978. *Bazzechi-Foto, Firenze.*
left The same in 1972. *Photo Peter Kinnear.*

3 *above* The bedroom after restoration in 1978. *Bazzechi-Foto, Firenze.*
right The same in 1972. *Photo Peter Kinnear.*

4A   The terrace. *Photo Peter Kinnear.*

4B   Ceiling of the little sitting room. *From a photograph made for the Linguistic Club of Florence.*

5 Tapestry. *From Sotheby catalogue, The Browning Collections, 1913.*

6   Elizabeth Barrett Browning, 1853, by Thomas Buchanan Read. *Courtesy of the Historical Society of Pennsylvania.*

7 Robert Browning, 1853, by Thomas Buchanan Read. *Courtesy of the Historical Society of Pennsylvania.*

8 Robert (*above left*) and Pen
(*left*) in 1860. Elizabeth (*above*)
in 1861. *Photo Alessandri,
Rome.*

9 *above right* Flush, a pen-
and-ink drawing by Elizabeth.
Courtesy of the Berg Collection.
right Pen and the pony. *From*
Letters of Robert Browning, *ed.*
T. L. Hood, Yale University
Press, 1933.
above Pen at the piano, a
watercolor by Fanny Haworth,
1858. *From Sotheran cata-*
logue no. 737.

Drawn the last time she ever sat under it. We left, the next day. RB.

1860. Oct. 7 – Villa Alberti Siena – My fig tree – EBB

10   A pen-and-ink drawing by Elizabeth, who signed it, "1860. Oct. 7 – Villa Alberti Siena – My fig tree – E B Browning." Robert added, "Drawn the last time she ever sat under it. We left, the next day. RB." *Sotheby catalogue, 1913.*

Aged five years & fifteen days

...nini's love to Mrs Page.

11 *above* A pencil drawing by Penini, "Aged five years & fifteen days," given to Mrs. William Page, who had been kind to him. *Courtesy of Arthur Sweeny, Jr. below* Another pencil drawing, perhaps by Peni at ten, of his father in a room of their rented flat. His mother has added their 1858–59 address, "43 V. Bocca di Leone. Ro[me.]" The drawing was given to Mrs. David Eckley. *Courtesy of the Berg Collection.*

XLIII

How do I love thee? Let me count the ways?
I love thee to the depth & breadth & height
My soul can reach, when feeling out of sight
For the ends of Being and Ideal Grace.
I love thee to the level of everyday's
Most quiet need, by sun & candlelight —
I love thee freely, as men strive for Right; —
I love thee purely, as they turn from Praise:
I love thee with the passion put to use
In my old griefs; and with my childhood's faith.
I love thee with the love I seemed to lose
With my lost Saints, — I love thee with the breath,
Smiles, tears, of all my life! — and if God choose,
I shall but love thee better after death.

12   Facsimile of Elizabeth Barrett Barrett's penultimate sonnet "from the Portuguese." *The British Library.*

Ferdinando Romagnuoli has been in my service for the last ten years, and only leaves it now in consequence of the cala=nitty which puts an end to my stay in Florence. I can give him the best of cha=racters for honesty, sobriety and kindli=ness of disposition: he is an excellent cook and knows the markets well both in Rome and Florence. He is accus=tomed to travel, has accompanied me to Paris and London, and can act as Courier if required. I recommend him strongly to anyone requiring a perfectly trust-worthy servant.

Robert Browning.

H. Enogat,
Britanny

Sept. 5. 1861.

13 Facsimile of Robert's letter of recommendation for Ferdinando. *Courtesy of John Murray and the Huntington Library.*

14 *above* The Villa Brichieri on Bellosguardo, Isa Blagden's home in Florence. *Francesco Pineider, Firenze.* *below* Elizabeth's monument in the Protestant Cemetery, Florence. *Photo by Mrs. Spurgeon B. Mallory, 1976.*

Bagni alla Villa
July 15 to October 10, 1853

For the summer of 1853, the Brownings returned to the Baths of Lucca where they rented the Casa Tolomei, house and garden. The house was large enough to provide Robert with a sitting room in which he worked hard at his poetry and to accommodate Robert Lytton as a house guest for two weeks. Elizabeth undertook Penini's spelling lessons. "D O G, dog; D O G, dog," she repeated patiently, as Penini repeated something else. "What a slow business," said Robert; and Elizabeth acquired a simile for *Aurora Leigh*:

> Men get opinions as boys learn to spell,
> By reiteration chiefly.

Life was much the same as it had been during their first stay at the *Bagni Caldi* in 1849 – teas, donkeys, gossip, and expeditions into the chestnut forests. The American sculptor William Wetmore Story, who was there with his wife and children, joined Elizabeth in experiments at table tipping. Robert "believes every other day," said Elizabeth.

A newcomer in the household was Ferdinando Romagnoli, engaged as replacement for Vincenzo of the unfortunate appearance. The new servant and Penini became at once "bosom friends," and their "mutual passion" was enhanced by the real gun Ferdinando brought with him from Florence. He had fought for the unification of Italy as a volunteer in the army of 1848, indicating satisfactory political views. One must presume that he was also satisfactory in appearance, odor, skill, and attitude, for he remained with the family till the end and received a fine *13* reference from Robert. Elizabeth hoped that he would "make Wilson comfortable." He did. In return, Wilson taught him how to make pea soup, Scotch broth, and her own North Country kneadcakes.

Casa Guidi
October 10 to November 15, 1853

The weather was quite cool when they left the *Bagni* for Florence, where they stayed only a month. A pleasant experience was going to the Pergola to hear Signor Verdi's "very passionate and dramatic" new opera, *Il Trovatore*. Unpleasant and tiresome, certainly, was sitting for their portraits by Thomas Buchanan Read, an American painter-poet then residing in Florence and now remembered for his poem "Sheridan's Ride" if not for his painting with the same title. Elizabeth would rather have had a portrait of Penini than of herself, but Robert insisted.

6, 7

Rome
November [22?], 1853 to May 28, 1854

After seven years in Italy, the Brownings made their first trip to Rome, where they spent the winter in a sunny flat at 43 Via Bocca di Leone. They reached the city after a "most exquisite" eight-day carriage trip by way of Assisi; father and son were "singing actually" as they passed through the Porta del Popolo in mid-November. On the morning after their arrival, the strangest notion got into Robert's head: without a word of warning, he shaved off his beard. Elizabeth wept when the shorn stranger walked in on her, and she ordered him to grow back the beard at once. He obeyed, but the new beard was tinged with gray. Elizabeth found the "argentine touch" "very becoming."

There was an interesting group of foreigners in Rome that winter: Thackeray and his daughters, Fanny Kemble, her sister Mrs. Sartoris, and the Duke of Wellington among the thousands of English. Among the four thousand Americans were the Storys, William Page (the "American Titian," who lived on a floor beneath the Brownings and who painted Robert's portrait), and Hatty Hosmer (a sculptress, whose *Clasped Hands* depicts Elizabeth's tiny hand enfolded in Robert's.) Mrs. Sartoris entertained at Friday musicales and at frequent picnics in the Campagna. Robert declined an invitation to act in a charade with the Kembles during Carnival, but he attended fourteen of their pic-

11

nics. On one such picnic, Fanny said to Robert, "You are the only man I have ever known who behaved like a Christian to his wife." (Robert had remained with Elizabeth when the other gentlemen bolted.) Peni was the only child among the forty adults Isa Blagden had in for quadrilles followed by fireworks sent aloft from her window. In black velvet frock and blue rosettes he dominated the group around him with a recitation declaimed from a sofa.

On Christmas morning the family attended mass at St. Peter's. Robert and Elizabeth had reserved seats, and she wore the *costume de rigueur*, black gown and black veil. In the public section, Ferdinando with Wilson at his side held Penini aloft to see the sights. Elizabeth was "much impressed and affected" and thought the music sublime. However, the "panting and shivering" of a table beneath her fingers at a *séance* had a "greater significance" than Michelangelo's basilica and the ritual therein. That evening at five they ate turkey and plum pudding at the Storys' house.

While Robert was out dissipating at parties – two or three of an evening sometimes – Elizabeth and Wilson stayed home and tried their hands at automatic writing. At one of the sittings, Elizabeth could feel the pencil turn in her hand with "a peculiar spiral motion," but the pencil would not write words or even letters for her. Wilson's pencil responded and wrote the name of her dead mother, for whom she was in mourning. Then Wilson's pencil wrote upside down and backwards so that Elizabeth across the table could read the name of her own mother – Mary Barrett.

Casa Guidi
June 1854 to June 20, 1855

On May 28, the Brownings began their trip from Rome to Florence by *vettura*. Their plan was to go to England in two weeks, but Elizabeth's ship money (dividends from her shares in the *David Lyon*), on which they had been counting, failed to materialize. They could not even afford to go to the mountains, so they remained happily in Florence through the beautiful months of spring, summer, and autumn, working hard at their poetry and hoping to take their publisher sixteen thousand lines between them when they could afford the trip to England.

As Penini flourished, Flush had been slowing down and appearing less and less in Elizabeth's letters. After all, he was fourteen (over ninety on the human scale). He had almost no hair, stank, and took no joy in life. One day in mid-June, Penini "screamed in anguish" when he came upon Flush, who had in the infirmities of age died quietly without pain. "A dear dog he was," Elizabeth said. They buried him in the cellar of Casa Guidi. The household no longer had a Flush, but Penini had six rabbits that he kept on his terrace, which Ferdinando cleaned every morning.

Elizabeth continued teaching Penini his books, and Robert continued teaching him music. She complained that "all those scales" were "rather dry" for her boy, and Robert countered that he did not interfere in her department. He knew that if he "pushed" Penini at the piano he could make an "infant wonder" of him in two years. In her department, she regretted that Penini could not spell. With Ferdinando and Wilson, Penini formed a family within the family. Every day they ate breakfast together, and Ferdinando usually had an extra treat for Peni, now fried eggs, now a deviled turkey leg, now a cutlet. Man and boy were often together in the kitchen singing "*La donna è mobile*" and other "scraps of operatic music." Elizabeth was gratified that when Penini could choose any gift he wanted, he chose not a gun or a toy soldier or a dagger, but a doll that squeaked and slept on a pillow beside him.

In the autumn an American dentist was in Florence, and American dentists, Elizabeth said, were "acknowledged by all nations to be sovereign in their art." Robert had four hour-long sittings for "stopping" (filling) several teeth and drawing one. In one half-hour sitting, the dentist drew five of Elizabeth's teeth and cleaned the remainder. For all this, he charged the poets only £2.

Winter came early with *tramontana* (north wind), frost, and snow. They moved the piano towards the windows and "packed" tables, chairs, and sofas close to the drawing-room fireplace. In January, Elizabeth suffered the worst "attack on the chest" she had had in Italy. Night after night Robert stayed awake, tended the bedroom fire, made coffee, and listened to her cough. Every night at ten he made her drink a tumblerful of asses' milk. In the spring the "divine weather" returned to Tuscany, and Elizabeth went out again, sometimes to church on Sunday.

They were up early working hard at their poetry. Robert spent four hours a day dictating his quota of completed lines to Isa Blagden, who prepared the fair copy for the printer. Between Penini's lessons and dinner at three, Elizabeth was well enough to work on her verse novel, which was far from complete. After dinner she "criticised" Robert's manuscripts and found the poems "magnificent." They did not show each other their unfinished poems, nor did either one read the letters the other wrote.

Elizabeth was also well enough to get into trouble. One day, when Hatty Hosmer and the Kinneys were visiting at Casa Guidi, Robert praised some pictures he had seen in a monastery from which women were excluded. Hatty, a light-hearted tomboy who had once derailed streetcars in her native Watertown, Massachusetts, leaped to her feet and proclaimed that they *would* go – disguised as male students, with Robert and Mr. Kinney as their tutors. Within a week they had rented boys' wigs and uniforms, which the ladies could hardly put on with the laughing. (This merry prank was in its way a realization of Elizabeth's girlhood dream to run away dressed as a man and become Lord Byron's page.) She was the first to be costumed, while the men went to fetch a *fiacre* to transport them all. As a safeguard against detection, the ladies were to enter the carriage inside the porte-cochere of Casa Guidi and drive unobserved to the monastery. Upon glancing out the window of the apartment, Hatty and Mrs. Kinney were stunned to see the most famous woman poet in the world, in her fiftieth year, walking up and down an Italian piazza, alone, and dressed like a man. Costumed and bewigged, they hurried down to her and were attracting the attention of amazed Florentines when their husbands arrived in the *fiacre*. They got the transvestites back into the house, a tearful Elizabeth afraid that they would go to jail, and an ashen Robert terrified lest their names appear in the paper. (Mr. Kinney was the U.S. Minister to the Court of Sardinia at Turin.) His wife attributed Elizabeth's "crazy act" and "wild deed" to an "extra dose of opium."

In May, Wilson and Ferdinando announced their engagement. The difference in their religions presented complications in Tuscany, where Wilson would have to agree to bring up their children as Catholics. Ferdinando was a lamb and would agree to any arrangement that Wilson and the Brownings wanted. He was rather Protestant than Catholic, and Wilson felt herself half an Italian. They decided to be married in Paris on their way to London, carrying with them a dispensation from the banns provided by the Archbishop of Florence.

Paris
June 24 to July 11, 1855

As in 1851, the Brownings left Casa Guidi for a year and a half to spend a summer in England, a winter in Paris, and a second summer in England before returning to Florence. They took ship from Leghorn to Corsica to Marseilles, where they learned that two of their boxes were missing in transit. It was maddening that one box contained the lovingly packed clothes – "pretty dresses, embroidered trousers, everything" – intended for Penini's London season. Fortunately, Elizabeth's brother Alfred was in Marseilles and he helped find the boxes and send them on after the poets to Paris. Ecclesiastical and civil red tape delayed the marriage of Ferdinando and Wilson until July 10. The next day the bride and groom left with their employers for their honeymoon in England.

London
July 12 to October 17, 1855

Mme. Romagnoli (née Elizabeth Wilson) waited as long as she dared before telling Elizabeth that she and Ferdinando were expecting a baby in October. The poets had suspected nothing,

even though Elizabeth especially was pleased with her own sophisticated knowledge of what she called the "economy of sex-
ual love" and was aware of "certain dangers" among servants.
Her first thought was, What would become of Penini without
Wilson?

The highlight of the summer was the *séance* conducted at Eal-
ing on July 23 by Donald Dunglass Home, the American medium *par excellence*. The poets "were touched by the invisible,
heard the music and raps, saw the table moved, and had sight of
the hands." Spirit hands lifted from the table a wreath of clema-
tis and placed it on Elizabeth's ecstatic head. She took the
wreath home, where it hung on her mirror until Robert threw the
hateful garland out the window.

On September 26 and 27, Tennyson paid "morning calls" on
them and stayed to dine with them, smoke with them, open his
heart to them, and consume "the second bottle of port" with
them. On the latter occasion, the laureate read aloud every single line of his *Maud*, interrupting at will with intercalary praise
of his own verse and keeping the Brownings up until three in the
morning. "If I had had a heart to spare," Elizabeth wrote, "certainly he would have won mine." Within the week she had "ex-
horted" Robert to smoke "occasionally." He refused.

Early in October a new maid, Harriet, was hired to replace
Wilson, who was sent off to her sisters in East Retford, and Elizabeth was glad when she was "fairly gone." Before departing,
she packed Elizabeth's clothes for the trip to the Continent.
Then, on October 17, the Brownings, Ferdinando, and Harriet
left for Paris, where news of the new baby came from East
Retford. On November 11, 1855, Oreste Wilson Romagnoli,
the son of Elizabeth and Ferdinando, a "courier of Florence in
Tuscany," was baptized in the Parish of East Retford, Nottingham, by Alfred Brook, Vicar.

Paris
October 18, 1855 to June 29, 1856

The flat reserved for them on the Rue de Grenelle was not successful, and they moved after six weeks to 3 Rue du Colisée, Avenue Champs Elysées. The six-year-old Penini missed Wilson and slept in his parents' bedroom – on the floor in the first flat and in his own bed in the second. On October 31, Elizabeth wrote to Arabel, "We have not yet heard Wilson's decision about coming or staying." The decision was whether to return to the Brownings and her husband in Paris or remain with her baby and sisters in East Retford. When she did ask to return, it was too late for Elizabeth to go back on her commitment to Harriet.

The flat on the Rue du Colisée provided a dressing-room–studio for Robert, who nevertheless wrote little or no poetry. His creative needs he fulfilled by drawing at the Louvre with his father or at home. Unlike Elizabeth, he could not relax with a light novel. As she lay on the sofa reading of an evening, he drew "some quite startling copies of heads."

The two volumes of *Men and Women* were published on November 11, and Robert had the experience, unusual for him, of seeing the expenses of publication covered by the sales of the first three days. But, alas, the sales soon fell off, for few realized that these volumes bound modestly in green cloth not only contained the fruit of Browning's first years of married life, but that they were also a high watermark in Victorian poetic achievement. Here was God's plenty: art poems to make us see, music poems to make us hear, religious poems to restore our faith, and love poems to remind us of first love. Fifty costumed men and women were allowed to have their say in fifty poems, with the poet himself often discernible beneath the costume. (Shakespeare allows his characters to reveal themselves, but Browning likes to expose his.) The companion poems this time were printed not side by side but in different volumes. Contemporary issues were boldly confronted on levels above and beyond the apparent ones.

Contemporary figures still exist behind the historical masks of the poems: Cleon is also Auguste Comte; Fra Lippo Lippi is also Robert Browning. What Brother Lippo says about art and artists or convention and break-through in Renaissance Italy parallels what Robert Browning behind the Lippo mask is saying about poetry and poets or critics and the reading public in Victorian England. Fra Lippo's companion poem in Volume II is "Andrea del Sarto (Called 'The Faultless Painter')." In poetry, Browning informed his readers that Andrea's "faultless" painting lacked "soul"; and later, in prose, Robert complained to Isa Blagden that one of Tennyson's deficiencies was that his latest idyll described "anything *but* the soul." It is not impossible that there is a Faultless Poet behind Andrea, none other than the laureate providing a neat balance to the Browning behind Fra Lippo.

Elizabeth worked like a fury, meanwhile, resolved to take eight books of *Aurora Leigh*, her "poetic art novel," to England in June and eager to make the new book good. She did not neglect Penini's lessons, and she received few visitors – none at all before four o'clock. One gauche visitor was "a raw intensely American American, who came into the room without gloves." He offended Elizabeth by saying that believers in the spirits were of "*one-horse power*," and her editorial comment was that he was of "one-ass power himself."

They delayed in Paris while Elizabeth raced to finish her poem, but it was not quite ready when they left for London on June 29.

England
June 30 to October 23, 1856

John Kenyon, who was on the Isle of Wight, lent them his London house at 39 Devonshire Place, where they settled down with two of his servants to clean and attend the house and with their own servants to cook and attend them. When they had readied the eleven thousand lines of *Aurora Leigh* for the printer, they left London for the Isle of Wight, taking Wilson with them. She had made the painful "decision." There was not room in the Browning household (or in other Victorian households) for a maid with a baby of her own. Wilson could have her son or her husband but not both. She decided to return to Elizabeth and Penini and Ferdinando and to leave her son with her sisters, to whom she would send money for the boy's support.

On the Isle of Wight, the Brownings joined Arabel at Ventnor for two weeks and then John Kenyon at West Cowes, visiting and reading proof at both places. Kenyon was very ill, dying indeed, and he was especially pleased when he saw Elizabeth's gracious dedication of *Aurora Leigh* to him. Finally, the family spent the week of September 22 with Henrietta at Taunton in Somerset.

It was eleven o'clock at night on the last day of September when the Brownings arrived back at Devonshire Place, where Ferdinando had a fire and a spread table cloth and an "eccellentissimo" ham awaiting them. Elizabeth was too tired to stop for even a bite of the ham, but a cup of hot tea followed her to her bedroom. Oreste Romagnoli had been brought down from Nottingham and was presented to his parents' mistress, who found him "a pretty, interesting baby of just a year, with great black Italian eyes." On October 23, Robert and Elizabeth left London and proceeded to Florence by way of Paris and Marseilles, with Wilson, Ferdinando, and Penini together again and Oreste with his aunts at East Retford.

Casa Guidi
October 30, 1856 to July 30, 1857

They found that their tenants had left the house "in excellent order" and that they had enough money to furnish the extra room that had been added to their renewal lease in 1850. The new furniture included chairs, sofa, and drugget carpeting for the floor. Robert had been using this spare room as a dressing room and would be more comfortable with a carpet "to save bare feet" as he trod "the chill scagliola bedward." At once he planned to raise the rent on future tenants. There was enough money to buy in addition a large looking glass and a new wardrobe for Elizabeth, as well as a new bed for Penini. His bed was placed at the foot of the ducal bed in his parents' room. In his eighth year, Peni no longer slept where Wilson had been his guardian angel, for Ferdinando was there guarding Wilson.

Elizabeth's *Aurora Leigh* appeared in November, exactly a year after Robert's *Men and Women*, and was extravagantly noticed: "the finest poem written in any language this century" (John Ruskin), "like the shriek of a railway whistle" (Coventry Patmore), and so on and so forth. The "mamas of England," shocked by the frank discussion of "The Woman Question," prostitution, seduction, brothels, dope, and rape, refused to let their daughters read it. Some of the verses were suitable for embroidering on the banners of marching militants:

> Must I work in vain,
> Without the approbation of a Man?
> It cannot be: it shall not.
>
> * * *
>
> . . . get work, get work.
> Be sure 'tis better than what you work to get.

There was undocumented talk that the book had been written by the spirits. It sold like mad.

John Kenyon died on December 3, leaving his largest bequest to the Brownings: £6,500 to Robert and £4,500 to Elizabeth. "If we had expected anything considerable, (but, as you know, we did *not*), there would have been some disappointment on our own part," Elizabeth wrote to Henrietta. (Mr. Kenyon died without including in his will the large fortune that his recently deceased brother had left him, with the result, Elizabeth pointed out, that the residuary legatees received £80,000 in addition to their specific legacies.) Invested in Tuscan untaxed government bonds at five per cent, the Brownings' inheritance produced £550 a year, which, added to the income from Elizabeth's English funds, her ship money, and their royalties, made them henceforth more than comfortable.

The poets were especially gay during Carnival. After Penini had "persecuted" Mama into buying him a blue domino and blue satin mask, he ran about the streets "talking Italian to strangers" with Wilson panting after him. The poets donned dominoes and went to a masked ball. Robert hired a box on the third tier at the opera for one night in order to return the hospitality of kind friends. He had a beautiful black silk domino made for himself, and at the last minute Elizabeth decided to go and hired one for herself. They arrived about ten-thirty, received their guests in their box, and then went down to mingle with the masked crowds at the ball below, as did the Grand Duke and the grandees. Elizabeth was pleased by the mingling of the classes, gratified by the display of "social equality," and delighted to observe the Grand Duke and Ferdinando "elbowing one another." Ever ready to make comparisons unfavorable to the English, she wrote home, "That such an expression of social equality should be possible, without offense to any class's delicacy; without rudeness, without coarseness, . . how remarkable! how instructive to an English man or woman!" At one o'clock Ferdinando served supper in their box: galantine, sandwiches, cakes, ices, and champagne. At two in the morning, Elizabeth took a carriage back to Casa Guidi. Robert carried on until half past four.

The gaiety came to an abrupt halt on Ash Wednesday, when everybody turned to sighing, fasting, and "enlarging their petticoats." In the 1850's, the Empress Eugénie had made the hoop skirt again fashionable, and a genius had invented the "hoop cage" of steel or whalebone to assure amplitude for the skirts and flounces ten yards in circumference. Elizabeth had Robert's domino made over into a beautiful black silk dress for herself and bought two "whalebone hoops," as well as a "tower of Malakoff" crinoline petticoat. She found the hoops "cool," as they were indeed after the horsehair petticoats they supplanted. The inventor of the cage made a million francs in less than a month, and for reasons of space the Pope had to ban the modish amplitude from St. Peter's Basilica.

Both poets paid much attention to their clothes, and Mrs. Jameson chided them for their obedience to fashion. Elizabeth liked dark colors – blues and blacks – and she was eager to wear hoops or bustles or umbrella hats or whatever was the *dernier cri*. Still, she had an old-fashioned look because she half hid her face with ringlets of "profuse feathery curls." (Elizabeth's large brown eyes, falling curls, and wistful expression suggested a spaniel to Mrs. Ogilvy, who detected a likeness to Flush.) Robert tormented his wife for the lace caps and the bonnets she preferred when other women wore hats or went uncovered in the evening. He did not know that her eyes had grown cavernous, her nose and mouth too prominent, and her chin too small; but she, who detested mirrors, knew and tried to conceal her worn features with the ringlets and bonnets of her girlhood. When Eugénie made hoop skirts the fashion in order (some said) to conceal her pregnancy, Elizabeth obeyed. But Elizabeth did not obey when the same Eugénie decreed that women wear their hair away from the face and forehead because she wished to reveal her own beautiful features. (Elizabeth was less than half joking when she ventured this motive for Eugénie's preferred coiffure and her own refusal to copy it.)

Robert was even more conscious of clothes than was Elizabeth. He had to have his own dressing room and never allowed anybody, even his wife or father, to see him in the process of robing. People thought he dressed less like a poet than like a banker or a butler or a dandy. Still, he could make mistakes: Carlyle suspected the young Robert of "scampery" because he called in a smart green riding coat. Elizabeth the bride winced whenever her groom appeared in his "unmentionable plaids." The mature widower was so meticulous about gloves that nobody ever saw him on the streets of London without them, but he would invite comment with a dazzling white waistcoat.

On April 17, Elizabeth's father died of erysipelas – unreconciled with those of his children who had married. Elizabeth was intensely Victorian in her morbid reaction to death. (Think of the Queen's behavior after the death of Albert.) Robert took over Penini's lessons, as his wife lay for weeks on the sofa, unable to stir or speak. At first she could not even cry. In due time Robert forced her off the sofa and out of the house to take carriage rides in the new mourning clothes she described to her sister: crepe sleeves and collar, black net and long ribbons for the hair, black cloth jacket, and silk shirt. She had not the heart to put Penini into mourning.

Bagni alla Villa
July 30 to October 7, 1857

On July 30, they took the railroad to Lucca, carrying with them a "mass of books" from the lending library. About ten in the evening they arrived at Casa Betti, where Mrs. Stisted had arranged that pigeon pie, tarts, and iced lemonade be spread for their arrival. Friends from Florence followed and put up at a local inn, the *Pellicano*. Every morning at six-thirty, Robert bathed in the rapid little mountain stream, and he rode mountain ponies mornings and evenings. Strong men carried Elizabeth about in a *portantina*, a sort of sedan chair. Casa Betti provided a "pretty good" piano but no studio or models for Robert's drawing. He began writing poetry again.

Peni returned from his first donkey ride "with his embroidery all in rags." Reluctantly Elizabeth relaxed her sartorial standards and ordered a pair of long white jeans for Peni to wear when riding donkeys. "Not for the world on other occasions." On other occasions, he continued to wear silk, velvet, embroidery, lace drawers, and feathers, even though he was becoming mutinous and wanted a haircut and clothes like other boys.

That summer the Brownings became intimate with a family of very wealthy Bostonians: David Eckley, his wife Sophie, and son Doady, who was Pen's age. Sophie was as sweet as she was wealthy and also a "powerful medium." Robert and David, who rode daily together, on one occasion set out at half past one in the morning to scale a famous mountain. Later in the day, Elizabeth and Sophie travelled twenty miles in a carriage and ten miles on donkeys to join their husbands for dinner. On that trip, Robert's pony fell "head over heels" down a precipice of sixty feet. Luckily a tree broke the fall, and Robert rescued himself by catching at a "crag of rock."

There was frightening gastric fever at the Baths that summer. Robert sat up nights at the *Pellicano* during the illness of young

Robert Lytton. Then Peni caught the fever, as did Annunziata, who had been summoned from Florence to replace Wilson, who had been in bed for a week and had to be sent back to Florence when "premature confinement" was expected. Robert thought that a husband and wife should not be separated, but Wilson could not be expected in her condition to minister to an invalid mistress. On August 29, she left the Brownings and her husband, "all in tears, poor thing." On September 1, she transmitted £12 (almost ten months' wages) to her sister Ellen in England for the support of her son Oreste. One wonders how she fared, ill and alone in Florence.

Annunziata gave the greatest satisfaction. She was, in Elizabeth's words, active, intelligent, good natured, kind, gay, and affectionate. "One of those enchanted new brooms," she was not only accomplished in hair-dressing and dress-making, but she could charm Peni with *novelle* about the devil and his pomps. ("Per Bacco!" said Elizabeth.) A "capital playfellow" for Peni, the new maid was known to run about the house blindfolded and appear in the drawing room "in a complete male costume, trowsers and all!!" as Peni shouted with laughter. Her wage was £3 a year less than Wilson's had been.

On October 7, Peni being well enough to travel, the family and servants returned to Casa Guidi.

Casa Guidi
October 7, 1857 to July 1, 1858

The winter was cold and uneventful. For the first time in a decade there was ice on the Arno. Elizabeth did "nothing but dream and read French and German romances." Robert rode for two or three hours a day and spent much time in the sculpture studio of Hiram Powers and in the studio of George Mignaty, where he watched the artist "draw from the nude." Three or four times a week he spent informal evenings at Isa Blagden's villa on Bellosguardo. Elizabeth gave about an hour a day to Peni's lessons, but, "afraid of wearing his brain," she let him spend most of his study time in Robert's department at the piano. He played "remarkably well," and Fanny Haworth painted a "quite lovely"

picture of him at the piano "looking like an inspired little
Mozart."

When Wilson left the Brownings' service, she rented a house
of her own next door to Casa Guidi, planning to supplement Ferdinando's wages by taking paying guests in a sort of *pensione*.
For a time, Fanny Haworth and another lady lodged with her. It
was in this house that Pilade Romagnoli, the second son, was
born on November 11, 1857. Two hours after the birth, Peni
was on the scene, his "enchantment" being "as if he were the
papa & mama both in one." Every day he called next door and
held the new baby on his knee. Fanny was the godmother when
Pilade was baptized on January 3 in the English church. (Whatever the terms of the Parisian marriage, it was clear that Wilson's sons were not to embrace their father's religion and that
their Christian names were to be pagan.) It was a grand conven-
ience to have Wilson next door to keep an eye on Casa Guidi
and to forward mail when the Brownings were away with Ferdinando and Annunziata.

Two days after Christmas, Peni was host at a party he had
planned for a month: hundreds of little wax torches ablaze on the
high stove and walls of his own rooms, a table spread with cakes
and wine, strings of pictures and toy soldiers. His guests included his boy friends, heaps of Italian girls – and Wilson. Not
yet eight, Peni planned to be married "in about twelve years"
and proposed to his mother.

Robert had become jumpy and excitable at any reference to
spiritualism or to D. D. Home, Elizabeth's "*protégé* prophet,"
who was then in Italy summoning spirits and laying ghosts. Robert was required to give his word that he would not kick Home in
the street should their paths cross. The subject of spiritualism
was taboo. Rebutting his wife's study of the occult, Robert pro-
cured a human skeleton for his studio and studied anatomy, not
sparing Elizabeth shuddering descriptions of the gutta-percha
joints and of how the head came on and off the fleshless bones. In
counter rebuttal, she declined to look at the skeleton.

In February, everybody had influenza. Peni caught the bug
and refused to stay in bed unless Pilade was placed on the pil-

low beside him. Elizabeth was convinced that there was no danger of infection, because Pilade had quite recovered from his own attack of flu. Robert also suffered from the "prevailing malady." After some persuasion from Elizabeth and Fanny Haworth and with his characteristic "smile of scorn," he tried homeopathy. Elizabeth had "a profound disbelief in the power & knowledge of medical men" and thought that "the medical art" was "the merest blind guessing." Homeopathy, however, was "a road broken in the right direction," comparable in its infinite possibilities to spiritualism and hypnotism. Homeopathy is defined as "a system of medical treatment based on the use of minute quantities of remedies that in massive doses produce effects similar to those of the disease being treated." Robert bought himself a treatise on the subject and a chest of medicine. As the treatise directed, he gave up tea, coffee, and wine, drinking prepared chocolate instead, and he became really devoted to *nux vomica*, taking the "globules in water," which was then "considered the strongest form." *Nux vomica* (emetic nut), from which strychnine is derived, is a foul-tasting digestive tonic thought to be good for constipation, bladder weakness, and other maladies. Prolonged use makes one jumpy and excitable, as Robert was anyway. He was "painfully subject" to "derangement of the bilious organs." But the *nux* did him the world of good, and his appetite was "wonderfully enlarged." His "irritability of the nervous system" was "calmed down" beyond all expectation, and his "liver quite relieved." Elizabeth makes frequent reference to the *nux* in her letters. Robert never does, but we know that thirty years later he was still taking small doses of strychnine every day.

In June, Nathaniel Hawthorne, his wife, three children, and their governess arrived in Florence. Son Julian, an American American, was contemptuous of Peni and his Little Lord Fauntleroy clothes. Governess Ada Shepard, a recent graduate of Antioch College in Ohio, proved skillful at automatic writing. She thought it well to abandon the experiments when evil spirits seized her pencil and shocked the company with some pornography unknown to a female graduate of Antioch, class of 1857.

Shortly before the Brownings left Florence for the summer, William Cullen Bryant and Hawthorne spent an evening with them at Casa Guidi.

Paris and Le Havre
July 6 to October 18, 1858

Ferdinando remained with Wilson and Pilade when the Brownings spent the summer of 1858 in France. They left Florence on July 1, Peni sobbing "with his shoulders" as he parted from his "bosom friend" at the railway station. The cabins were so stuffy on the ship from Leghorn to Genoa that Elizabeth of the spring sofas and down pillows spent the first night on deck, sleeping on bare planks between Robert and Peni. Thanks to *nux vomica*, Robert was "in a heavenly state of mind" when they arrived in Paris. There they joined his father and sister and for two weeks enjoyed the French cuisine that Robert loved.

The next two months they spent by the sea at Le Havre with Robert's father and sister, visited some of the time by Elizabeth's sister Arabel and two of her brothers. Elizabeth took "much more of a bath" than had been recommended by her doctor in Florence. Every morning a hipbath in her bedroom was filled with lukewarm sea water, and she was immersed in it from five to eight minutes. Robert was slow to bathe, saying that he felt bilious. He never went into the sea in England, where sexually segregated Victorians bathed in the nude, but the French wore bathing costumes, and after Robert had one made, he and Pen bathed every day. (He remained apprehensive, though, that some "clownish person" might throw open the door of the bathing machine in which he was undressing.) On September 20, they returned to Paris for three weeks. Of course they went shopping. Elizabeth bought a bonnet, a parasol, and a red and black warm petticoat. Robert bought an artist's mannikin and a single opera glass "of great power" for thirty francs. Then they undertook the nine-day journey back to Florence.

Casa Guidi
October 26 to November 18, 1858

It was summer when they arrived in Florence, but in a few days winter surprised them with cold and snow and then rain. They stayed in Casa Guidi a bit less than a month, during which time Robert commissioned for Elizabeth a bust of Peni by Alexander Munro at a cost of twenty-five guineas, which sum would pay the Casa Guidi rent for a year or Ferdinando's wage for twenty months. Elizabeth thought the bust "exquisite in the clay" and, if money was the question, "would rather have given up Rome and had the bust." It was to be exhibited in the marble in London. Wilson thought it "too melancholy" for Peni.

Wilson found courage to venture a modest proposal calculated to unite her flock. She would return to Elizabeth's service, send for her sister to take care of the lodging-house and children in Florence, and she and Ferdinando would go to Rome with the Brownings. Elizabeth conceded that it was natural for a wife to want to be with her husband, but how could Wilson ask her to be so unjust to Annunziata? Oreste remained in England with his aunts; Wilson and Pilade remained in Florence; and Ferdinando spent the winter in Rome with the Brownings and Annunziata.

For days they had been packed and ready to leave, but "weather-bound, wind-bound, snow-bound," they could not take to the road. Sophie Eckley, who had fallen in love with Elizabeth "for spiritual concordances and other worse reasons," implored the Brownings to take one of the two Eckley carriages, paying only for the expenses of the horses. Ferdinando was sent on ahead with furnishings for the winter, including plate and linen. He went by rail to Leghorn, by sea to Civita Vecchia, and thence on to Rome. Suddenly in mid-November, Tuscany was "transfigured back into summer," and the two families could begin their seven-day journey to take up residence in Rome for the winter.

Alla Vettura
November 18 to 24, 1858

Travellers who today go from Florence to Rome by train *direttissimo* in a couple of hours might envy the Brownings the leisure of their journey. The speediest journey in 1858 took thirty-six hours by diligence, but one would have to be hardy to travel that way. In a carriage, one could go by way of Siena in five or six days, but the Brownings chose the more scenic route by way of Arezzo and Perugia, spending seven days and six nights on the road. At intervals of about eight miles on their route, there were twenty-seven posts where travellers could change horses, dine, and in some places spend the night.

They left Florence on Thursday morning in a "blaze of sunshine," the rains having washed away all the snow in Italy. The Eckley party in the open barouche included Mrs. Tuckerman (Sophie's mother) as well as coachman, courier, and maids. The Browning party in the closed carriage with open windows included the coachman on the coach box with Annunziata beside him, and Robert, Elizabeth, and Peni within among the cushions. Wilson saw them off in tears.

They travelled some forty miles a day, stopping at noon for two hours and a second breakfast of eggs, tea, and coffee. Then they continued their journey till early evening, when they dined and went straight to bed. Elizabeth had plenty of books to read in the carriage and no "over-talking" to vex her. She and Sophie found occasion to communicate with the spirits and to translate some love poems of Heine for each other. Sophie treasured this translation:

> The years they come & go
> The races drop in the grave
> Yet never my love doth so
> Which, for thee, in my heart I have.
> Might I see thee but once, one day
> And sink there down on my knee

And die in thy sight while I say
'Madam, I love but thee'?

Heine

Nov. '58   *Ba* for Sophia

On Friday they passed through Arezzo on the way to Camuscia, where they spent the night. That day their spirited horses rebelled and one pulled the other into a ditch, the carriage "just escaping." The coachman jumped down, leaving Annunziata on the coach box "dragging wildly at the reins and shrieking at the top of her voice." The Eckley courier came back to assist them, and all was righted.

The same thing happened the next morning as the party descended a mountain, but this time the horses attempted to drag the carriage over a precipice instead of into a ditch. Annunziata leaped from the coach box, opened the door of the carriage, and all were out in a moment. The Eckleys then lent their courier to sit beside the Brownings' coachman and took Annunziata with them. The horses were led down the mountain to the neighboring town, and all was well thereafter. That night the party slept in Perugia.

More adventure awaited. They engaged oxen teams to haul the carriages up a mountain, and two of the oxen drivers got into a fight. When one attempted to stab the other, Robert rushed between them and was knocked to the ground. Peni shrieked, "They are going to kill Papa!" and Elizabeth all but fainted. Robert's trousers were torn, but peace was re-established, and slowly the indifferent oxen pulled the carriages up the mountain.

Sunday night they slept in Spoleto, and on Monday they cut their journey short at Terni in order to see the falls. There were April showers that day as there had been on Sunday, and Elizabeth and Sophie preferred to stay behind while Robert, David Eckley, and Mrs. Tuckerman visited the torrential cascades, which were all the more impressive since the rain and melted snow had greatly increased the supply of water. It was fortuitous that they did stop at Terni, for on the road they would have taken and at the time they would have been there, *banditi* attacked a carriage and robbed a gentleman and his wife of sixty-two scudi.

On Tuesday they went from Terni to Civita Castellana, and on Wednesday on to Rome, where they arrived at the Porta del Popolo at four in the afternoon to find a smiling Ferdinando awaiting them. They spent the first night at the new and inexpensive Hotel d'Angleterre.

Rome
November 24, 1858 to May 25, 1859

The Rome of 1858 was very like the Rome of their first visit in 1853. They rented the same apartment on the Via Bocca di Leone, which, newly cleaned, painted, and carpeted, cost ten Roman dollars more per month than it had cost five years earlier. Home life was much the same: Peni played the piano; Elizabeth took morphine; and Robert took *nux*. Almost every day he said that he preferred an evening at home with his wife, and almost every evening he went out. What "dancing & dining, & crowding!" "Such reckless dissipation!" "Paris is quiet and solemn in comparison to Rome," she said, adding that she "liked to see Robert so perfectly amused." Despite the evening dissipation, he rose in the dark before six every morning and walked with David Eckley into every corner of Rome. He wrote no *Men and Women*.

Sophie Eckley called on Elizabeth almost every day, and often the two women attempted to communicate with the spirits. Sophie was a "powerful medium" indeed, but Elizabeth was taken aback sometimes when English spirits used "certain Americanisms" in transmitting their messages through Sophie. She always came bearing the most expensive gifts, until Elizabeth feared to admire anything at all lest it be presented to her the next day. Sophie deeply treasured the gift she received from Elizabeth in return: "A flower from the grave of Keats."

In Rome, they did as the Romans did and dined at five o'-clock. "Robert never dines out now," said Elizabeth, "*except*

11

when he does." There was often an excuse to go, and he returned with descriptions of Lucullan meals, such as the roast porcupine he ate at Mr. Cartwright's. When he accepted an invitation to dine on "the delicate luxury of a whole dinner 'dressed in garlic' in company with Lady William Russell," Elizabeth considered the advisability of a separation. "Avert the nose of your imagination," she wrote to Henrietta. He ate "vulpinely." He put on weight. Annunziata was required to let out his waistband.

Elizabeth stayed home in their "poky" rooms on the third floor, avoiding the cold that covered the fountains with shaggy icicles. She did attend high mass at St. Peter's on Christmas Day, "thrilled through" her "bones" by the blast of silver trumpets and impressed by the presence of two kings, not to mention the Pope and cardinals. She and Sophie Eckley, in black dresses and veils, sat in the reserved section with Peni. Robert and David Eckley stood in the crowd. During this stay in Rome, the poets went to Catholic services and no others. "I did prefer St. Peter's & the like," she wrote to Arabel, "& have enjoyed few *modes* of worship so much as that gathering together in the solemn twilight of the aisles, with the sublime music floating upwards with my prayers." Both she and Robert "liked it extremely," yet they were "far from being RC's." She had shaken off her early trammels and could now assist at an entire Roman Catholic mass without once thinking of the "Scarlet Lady." "Robert's fault," she told Arabel, "was his intolerant protestantism expressed often too vehemently." Her thought was that "all these church walls, English, Scottish, Roman, equally must all be swept away, before Christ can be seen standing in the midst."

In February she went to see William Page's *Venus*. Though a Victorian and dissenting English female, the author of *Aurora Leigh* was far more liberated than the male French directors of the Paris Exhibition. They refused to exhibit the painting "on the ground of nudity," whereas the only indecency Elizabeth found was in the *face*. On February 25, Robert dined with Albert Edward, Prince of Wales, having earlier been informed that

Queen Victoria would find it "gratifying" that the Prince "should make Mr. Browning's acquaintance." Elizabeth instructed Robert to "set them all right on Italian affairs," and he did. He held forth on the "wrongs of Italy," and the seventeen-year-old prince was "evidently sympathetic." The heir apparent evidenced his sympathy by listening intently and making no comment.

During this stay in Rome, both Brownings sat to several artists for companion portraits, the most satisfactory of these being the chalk drawings by Field Talfourd. Ellen Heaton (Fanny Haworth's friend) commissioned the Talfourd portrait of Elizabeth for a fee of £20 and tactlessly said that she was going to have "the only portrait in the world of Mrs. Browning," rather pointedly disparaging the Gordigiani half-length in oils that Sophie Eckley had commissioned in Florence. (Some of the women in Elizabeth's circle tempered their love of her with jealousy of each other.) Elizabeth knew that the Talfourd flattered her without restraint, but Robert considered it "the best in existence, perhaps." He had photographic copies made to give to friends and then sat to Talfourd himself.

Elizabeth received afternoons from four to five, and sometimes twenty or more visitors called in the course of a *soirée*. She served no food but sat on the sofa and poured tea, which Ferdinando passed about. Her intense desire for the unification of Italy approached hysteria, and she was, therefore, more exhilarated by a visit from the patriot Massimo d'Azeglio than by Robert's dinner with the Prince of Wales. Edward Lear was received a few times, unfavorably impressed by the sycophancy of the other guests. Not everybody was adulatory. Julia Ward Howe, whom Elizabeth had vexed, wrote "Kenyon's Legacy," a poem in which she avers that people called on the Brownings expecting refreshments but all they got was divine talk.

Casa Guidi
Early June to July 30, 1859

After their return to Florence about June 1, Elizabeth professed to be tired of hearing people say that she looked well. Scarcely ever in her life had she been so happy. She felt as if "she walked among the angels of a new-created world." Italy was at war and driving out the foreign despots. Unification was just around the corner. On May 12, Elizabeth's hero Louis Napoleon had landed at Genoa with French troops and had joined the Italian armies in a series of victories over the Austrian invaders. Leopold II, the Austrian Grand Duke of Tuscany, shrugged and abdicated. Napoleon and Victor Emmanuel entered Milan in triumph. The Empress Eugénie named her favorite color after the allied victory at Magenta.

Robert contributed two guineas a month to the war, and Peni contributed the coins he received in reward when he did his lessons well. On the terrace of Casa Guidi, he hung two flags, one French and one Italian, and he made forays into the camp of the French soldiers in the Cascine, thrilled when he saw them playing blindman's buff.

There were a few grace notes for Elizabeth: Austrian Prince Metternich died; the correspondent at Rome to the infamous *Times* of London contracted Roman fever; and nearly all the Continental English fled.

The heat was ferocious that summer, 102 degrees in the shade on occasion, but the Brownings would not leave Florence for any retreat where they would not have instant access to the war bulletins issued twice a day. Forgetting that she was an invalid, Elizabeth found herself going out a great deal. They saw Salvini in *Hamlet* and *Othello*. They called on people. In her "excitement and exultation" Elizabeth did not give a thought to what might happen to their £11,000 invested in the Tuscan funds. "But I did," Robert said.

When the Brownings returned to Florence, they found that Wilson had gone "quite mad," religiously insane. She was convinced that the baker was trying to poison her, and she made a great to do about getting a precise coin, *not the equivalent*, back from Fanny Haworth's maid. Wilson's study of the Bible had convinced her that the end of the world was at hand, that she and Ferdinando were "too near in blood" for cohabitation, that he was to marry someone else, that her sons were "the first fruit of the first resurrection," and that a virgin was again to produce a child. In confirmation of her exegesis, she was to see an angel carry her son Oreste past the house. Elizabeth advised her to stop reading the New Testament. "All was just as clear in the Psalms," said Wilson.

Her business was beginning to pay, and she had hired a maid, Teresa, to help her. However, it would not be good for the *pensione* if word got round that the landlady was crazy. Again and again Wilson asked to return to service, but how could a maid be at Elizabeth's beck and Peni's call while tending a child of her own? Her husband might be in Florence only two months of the year. For ten months of the year he was away with the Brownings and Annunziata, and Wilson had proof positive that Ferdinando had a way with a maid. Elizabeth gives no hint of suspicion that being separated from her husband while obliged to rear his child and operate a business in a foreign country might drive a woman mad. Elizabeth suspected rather that weaning the baby was the cause.

On a ferociously hot day in July, Robert ran into Walter Savage Landor on the street in a rage. The white-maned poet in his eighty-fifth year had walked out on his quarrelsome wife, Julia, vowing never to return to their villa in Fiesole. Landor, now, was not one to trifle: the last time he had walked out he had stayed away for twenty-three years. (It needs to be said that, despite her viraginity and his intransigence, Landor was unfaithful to Julia only once, and in youth at that.) Robert took the lion to Casa Guidi and then got in touch with his wife in Fiesole and his brothers in England. Eventually she sent "the old Brute" a peasant's corn bag stuffed with his clothes, and they allowed £200 a year for his keep. Robert, "perpetual guardian," took Landor to Siena, where the Storys risked tending an active volcano as houseguest in their villa.

Just when Elizabeth's hopes for Italy were at their height and "rising into triumph," she received two crushing blows. She and Robert went to the Trollopes' house, where they saw a document professing to be from the Grand Duke ordering his troops to bomb the city of Florence. She suffered her "worst attack" in Italy, not only with the cough but with "violent palpitations" and the symptoms of *angina pectoris* for two days and two nights. (T. A. Trollope later wrote that the Grand Duke never gave such an order.) Just as Elizabeth's brave troops were winning victory after victory, Napoleon and the Emperor of Austria met at Villafranca near Verona and signed an infamous armistice. The Pope was to rule an Italian federation including Venetia; the Austrians were to retain Mantua; the Grand Duke was to return to Florence; and Italy was to remain dismembered. Napoleon III was no longer her hero but a cynical opportunist. She took to her bed, and for three weeks Robert went without sleep, caring for her through her tortuous nights disturbed by "political dreams." At the sound of the first gun, the English physicians had vanished, and Elizabeth was in the care of Dr. E. G. F. Grisanowsky, a German whom the Brownings knew socially. (Incidentally, Leopold II was sick and tired of being asked to leave the Pitti Palace, then to return, then to leave, and then to return. He had an immense personal fortune, lived modestly, and did not need the job. This time he let his eldest son be Grand Duke, and he retired to peace and quiet.)

Siena
July 30 to October 10, 1859

On July 30 Elizabeth was carried from the house to a carriage, from the carriage into the train for Siena, and from the train to the hotel, where they stayed for two days. Dr. Grisanowsky followed "uninvited," administered to his patient, and, unlike English physicians, refused recompense. He also helped Robert to find and rent the beautiful Villa Alberti at Marciano some two miles outside Siena. Count Alberti, "a fiery-haired, hook-nosed, fair-speeched man," was Robert's match in bargaining. When "they" gave Robert the two-months' lease to sign, he learned (1) that he had not rented the second floor, (2) that the rent was payable in advance, (3) that the *francesconi* agreed upon had become *scudi* (like pounds becoming guineas), and (4) that he had been "mulcted" out of two dollars. He signed, nevertheless, and they moved in on August 1.

"Air, quiet, and asses' milk" did more for Elizabeth than the hot blisters that the doctor prescribed for her side. She still had to be carried from bed to sofa, but within the week she was able to consume "a canary bird's allowance of toast" and later some "minced chicken." Better for her health than the solid food was her reassessment of Louis Napoleon. Upon reflection, she came to the conclusion that he had fought with personal courage, had negotiated the best terms possible at Villafranca, and had freed Italy "*potentially*" from north to south. After six weeks on the sofa, she went out on September 8 for an hour's ride in the carriage Robert rented.

Whenever Elizabeth took to the bed, Robert took over Pen's lessons. Pen, aged ten, worked at his books an hour a day, at the piano two hours a day (with Robert as maestro, he was studying Beethoven's *Sonata in Eb*, Opus 7), and rode his pony "like the wind" three hours a day. Robert had bought Pen a Sardinian pony whose tail was exactly the color of the boy's golden curls and had hired a second man-servant (a middle-aged cousin of Ferdinando's) to take care of the animal. Hamilton Wild, an American artist who was staying with the Storys, painted a portrait of Pen mounted.

Elizabeth remonstrated with Robert for having discontinued his morning walks, conceding that he was exhausted from sitting by her sick bed through the nights and mornings. He was "in very good looks altogether," and amused himself by letting his beard and moustache grow together. She thought the effect "picturesque."

The Brownings received in rotation houseguests of all classes: lower – "Wilson & her tribe"; middle – Isa Blagden and Kate Field; upper – Odo Russell. Odo was the nephew of Lord John and the son of Lady William Russell. He was unusually knowledgeable about music, for he thought Pen's performance "quite amazing." He was less knowledgeable about Italian affairs although in the diplomatic service of the Queen at the papal court.

During the three weeks Landor stayed with the Storys, his behavior was irreproachable and "courtly," disproving beyond reasonable doubt his virago wife's charge that he was "mad" and "ungovernable." He put himself into a good humor by sitting under the cypresses and composing Latin alcaics blasting his wife and Louis Napoleon. After he moved to his own house close to the Villa Alberti, he convinced himself that the servants opened his desk drawers, put poison in his tea, and conspired to slit his throat while he slept. When the Brownings returned to Florence, they took him back there with them.

Casa Guidi
October 10 to November 28, 1859

The Storys and Hamilton Wild had been so gracious during the summer that Elizabeth simply *had* to have them in for dinner. Robert objected to all dinner guests for the good reason (he said) that Ferdinando did not know how to arrange the table and for the better reason (he left unsaid) that Robert did not know how to carve. At a dinner in the proper English manner, all the food, except the entrées, was placed on the table at once with much reaching and leaning to right and left as the host carved and the arms of servants intruded between the diners. Elizabeth surmounted the inadequacies of her two men by having the dinner served *à la Russe*. When the company sat down, the only decorations on the table were piles of fruit and flowers arranged by Annunziata. Ferdinando carved at the side table, and Annunziata passed the dishes round. Robert did not have to carve, and nobody had to wait for anything. Pleased with her elegant success as hostess, Elizabeth had the Storys and Mr. Wild for dinner again.

Robert arranged for Landor to live with Wilson and lent her some money to enable her to rent a second house, this one on the Via Nunziatina (later 93 Via della Chiesa) on a side street not far from Casa Guidi. It was a small house directly behind the Church of Santa Maria del Carmine. Wilson, Pilade, and Teresa, the servant girl, lived on the ground floor; Landor on the first floor, where he had three rooms, a book closet, and a small terrace; and the landlord's son on the floor above Landor, who was to pay £1 a week rent and pay Wilson £30 a year for his care. She was also to have the leftovers from his meals sent in from a *trattoria*. The diminutive, soft-spoken lady's maid with a soul less stout than a "grasshopper's" was asked to manage the massive, booming old genius for the last five years of his life.

When Wilson's predecessor, Crow, had left Miss Barrett's service, Elizabeth had presented her with a handsome gift of money. When Wilson left the Brownings' service, she received only a loan to help her with her lodging house, and perhaps she "may have expected more" than a loan. But Elizabeth would not think of charging Wilson with "ingratitude." If she could rent her other lodging house (the one next door to Casa Guidi), she would have, from all sources, an income of £100 a year, Elizabeth reckoned.

At ten, Peni had not yet begun Latin, but he spent an hour a day at the piano with Signor Del Bene and another hour with Robert. He was studying Schuloff's *Carnaval de Venise*. How those small fingers could run and leap! One day he would be somebody in music. One night he fastened some string to his bed and his parents' bedpost, saying he was now "tied next to Mama." Elizabeth read three newspapers a day, avoided conversation, and was sometimes carried up the stairs to the apartment sitting on a "queen's cushion," constructed when Robert and Ferdinando interlocked their hands and wrists. Annunziata worked like three, never had a male visitor, and went out little. She even volunteered to do the ironing in Rome to save some of the laundry expenses. Wilson bore her a grudge, partly perhaps because of the satisfaction she gave, but especially for her proximity to Ferdinando. Wilson now had room in her house for Oreste, but how get him from England to Florence?

Before the household departed for Rome for the winter, Landor's rooms had been painted, carpeted, and furnished. Elizabeth paid a call and approved. Although Robert himself was not a penny out of pocket, his attention to Landor was most affecting. Everybody benefited: Wilson had an assured income; Landor had somebody to look after him; and Mrs. Landor did not have "the old Brute" under her feet in Fiesole.

Rome
December 3, 1859 to June 4, 1860

They took novels by Balzac and Charles Reade to pass the time on the six-day trip to Rome. Hitched to the carriage horses, Pen's pony trotted with the best of them "like a glorified Houyhnhnm," and on December 3 arrived in Rome "not merely fresh but fat." They stopped briefly at the Hotel d'Angleterre until they found a sunny flat on the second floor at 28 Via del Tritone. Because of the fear of war, Rome was a "solitude," rents were cheap, and Robert had less opportunity to dissipate evenings. There seemed to be more Americans than English there that winter, regulars like Charlotte Cushman, Hatty Hosmer, and the Storys, augmented by visitors like Harriet Beecher Stowe and Theodore Parker. Miss Cushman lent space in her stable for Pen's pony, stunningly groomed by Ferdinando's cousin.

The editors of the New York *Independent* offered Elizabeth $100 for every poem she would send them, and she sent them eleven lyrics, most of them on Italian affairs. The *Atlantic Monthly* asked both poets for poems "at any price," but Robert never liked to publish in periodicals.

Elizabeth received a few callers in the day time, and spent some time preparing Pen for his tutor, a "young and gentle" Abbé who was teaching Latin to Pen for less than what it cost to maintain his pony. "Although an Abbé & a priest," he seemed to Elizabeth "one of the most innocent & amiable of men." Robert wrote a good deal – some short lyrics that she liked and "a long poem" that he did not show her.

The poets ran a sort of subversive café in their apartment. The Roman authorities were intolerant of literature that advocated their own overthrow, but there were ways to get around the prohibitions. Isa Blagden would send books from Florence by diplomatic courier, or cause a seditious newspaper to be disguised as an innocent newspaper and mailed direct to the

Brownings. Ferdinando's friends came, often six at a time, to read the banned journals. Elizabeth guessed that she and Robert were suspected by the postal authorities, but "the freely breathed word" was made available to Tuscan exiles, and one day Italians would possess the liberties enjoyed by every individual in England, Ireland, Scotland, and Wales. Ferdinando would be as free to read the Bible as was his English wife.

Isa moved down into Casa Guidi when it became impossible to heat her large villa on Bellosguardo. Writing from Rome, Elizabeth explained how to close off the large drawing room and light a "regular bonfire" in the morning. Once heated, the room could be kept liveable through the day. (When the Brownings' lease for Casa Guidi was forwarded to Rome for renewal, they noted that their landlord, "in a spasm of terror at the idea of losing" them, had lowered the annual rent by almost twenty per cent.) Isa sent news of Landor. The old gentleman was intractable enough, and gentle Wilson was not gifted with the vituperative virtuosity of Mrs. Landor. When Wilson looked at the pictures he had hung on his walls, something came over her, and her old hallucinations returned.

Elizabeth's *Poems before Congress*, published in March, was "a little 'brochure' of [eight] political poems," a "thin slice of a little book" containing more bombshells than poems. English readers were informed that Napoleon III was the "Sublime Deliverer" of Italy and that thwarting English politicians were something else. English reviewers obliged with the abuse she wanted and interpreted as "the justification of the poems." Robert was *"furious"* at the *Athenaeum*. He never had loved and never would love reviewers. When he later returned to live as a widower in London, he kept in his back garden two pet geese that he named *Edinburgh* and *Quarterly* after those offenders. The silly birds would cackle and waddle toward him for their supper when he called them by name.

Casa Guidi
June 9 to July 7, 1860

They arrived back in Florence on June 9. Elizabeth and the pony were overtired by the swift carriage trip they had undertaken before completing their journey by rail. Pen had blossomed, and Robert was stout and robust as never before. Elizabeth thought his "*robustness*" the result of Rome or the *nux vomica*, to which he had been constant for two and a half years. He was in a good enough humor to let her have the *Spiritual Magazine* from England, and he "shouted in triumph" when the magazine scourged her political poems and affirmed that she was "biologised by infernal spirits."

Landor exploded into Casa Guidi one day with the report that Wilson had thrown a dish in his face and that he was leaving for Leghorn. "Her eyes flashed fire," he said. Wilson followed to report that his dinner from the *trattoria* had arrived eight minutes late and that he, according to his custom, had thrown it out the window. First went the soup, then the vegetables. With unprecedented spunk, she had snatched his mutton and her leftovers from him just as he was ready to throw that dish out. Robert used "every sort of rhetoric" on Landor, who agreed to pardon Wilson. Elizabeth instructed Wilson *not* to get "into a passion" and to endure "any extravagance," but Wilson said that something entered into her when he irritated her. (Elizabeth thought it inexcusable when Teresa quit one fine day without giving Wilson notice.)

On a scorching day this month, Robert paid eightpence for an old square yellow book at a second-hand stall in the Square of San Lorenzo. The book is in fact a collection of boring pamphlets bound together in vellum and dealing with a sordid murder case in seventeenth-century Rome. He was ever interested in the psychology of crime, violence, swift vengeance, and murder, and, as his wife observed, he had "a belief of the wickedness of human nature deep in him." At some risk to life and limb, he read the book from cover to cover as he walked through the busy streets from the square to Casa Guidi. Eight years later

Robert published *The Ring and the Book*, his masterpiece that converts the sordid pamphlets into 21,116 lines of blank verse.

Siena
July 7 to October 11, 1860

The Storys, the Brownings, and Landor returned to their former houses in Siena for the summer, and Wilson went along to look after Landor. Pen had his pony, his piano, and the Abbé. The Abbé instructed Pen and Edith Story in Latin; and Pen, aged eleven, instructed the Abbé in the infamies of Pope Pius ix. Pen worked harder with Edith as a rival.

It was a joy that Robert rode three or four hours a day, allowing Elizabeth to lie "at length on a sofa, in an absolute silence, nobody speaking for hours together . . . not a chance of morning visitors, no voices under the window." From the library in Florence she had books in which to lose herself. Journals, newspapers, and political pamphlets catered to one passion; the *Spiritual Magazine* to the other. Her hopes for Italy now centered in Camillo Benso di Cavour, whom she called, "that great soul, which meditated and made Italy."

Night after night, Robert went over to the Storys' villa where he sat with them on the terrace and talked until midnight. Sometimes they went indoors, where they played and sang together at the piano.

The gods seemed to have relented in their persecution of Wilson and propitiously provided a way to return Oreste to her from England. When the Ogilvys had left Florence for Scotland, they had taken with them an Italian nursemaid named Gigia, who in the summer of 1860 was returning to Florence. Oreste in his fifth year spoke no Italian, whereas Pilade two years younger spoke no English. What irony that being so named, the brothers did not know and love each other like their mythical namesakes. Arrangements were made for Gigia to stay a few days with the Wilsons at East Retford, then to take Oreste to Liverpool, Marseilles, and Leghorn, where Ferdinando would meet their ship and take his son to Siena. Mr. Ogilvy would accompany them as far as Marseilles. Ferdinando went to Leghorn to find Gigia without his son, whose English aunts had refused to part with the boy. When Ferdinando brought the news to Wilson, she almost dropped to the ground in shock. He swore that he would send no more money to England for Oreste's support.

Casa Guidi
October 11 to November 18, 1860

A cloud hung over the family during this month spent in Florence. Word had come from England that Elizabeth's sister Henrietta, who was the mother of three children, was suffering from what proved to be terminal cancer. Every letter might bring bad news. Elizabeth asked herself whether she should go home.

Arabel was a bit concerned about what might happen to the Tuscan funds in time of war, whereas Elizabeth was concerned about their English funds. England was spending so much on national defense that the income tax might be raised, and taxes were minimal in Tuscany. She made "unpatriotic" inquiry about transferring the English funds, if the trustees of the marriage settlement could and would approve. The English funds paid only three per cent less taxes, whereas the untaxed Italian funds paid five per cent. She told her brother that she would rather have her money finance a war to free Venetia than finance fortresses on the Thames.

The doctor had advised Elizabeth not to spend another winter in Florence. Much as she wanted to watch the post for news about Henrietta, Robert insisted that they depart for Rome before it became too cold to travel. There would be no news during the journey, and bad news could be forwarded.

Rome
November 23, 1860 to June 1, 1861

They lived at 126 Via Felice during their last winter in Rome. On December 3 came the news that Henrietta had died on the Friday evening of their arrival in Rome. In grief, Elizabeth could neither talk nor cry. The first thing "from without" that did her good was a letter from America in which Harriet Beecher Stowe wrote that she had communicated five times with her dead son through different mediums ranging from "high Calvinists" to "low infidels."

Elizabeth did not go out to pay one call throughout the winter, but some visitors climbed her stairs. Annunziata thought that Lady Juliana Knox had a name that sounded like Robert's medicine. Sir John Bowring came to talk politics. Elizabeth heard that English "volunteers" in Naples "left the worst impression of English morals." They came home "dead drunk," and the drunkenness was not "the worst," whatever the worst was. She observed that Italians (perhaps Ferdinando's patriot friends) were franker talking to her alone than they were when Robert was present. What she heard about Cavour and his policies heartened her hopes for Italy.

Robert's "irritable nerves" and "enormous superfluity of vital energy" required that he be occupied, as he was several hours a day in Story's sculpture studio, where he made "extraordinary progress" in modelling in clay, making copies of classical works – busts and "a perfect copy of a small torso of Venus," which he brought home to Elizabeth. Nothing had ever made him so happy before, and he said that "all his happiness" lay in clay now. Although he did not write poetry, he had from the previous winter "material for a volume," which Elizabeth read and which appeared in 1864 entitled *Dramatis Personae*.

After Elizabeth went to bed at eight, her husband went out as a bachelor and came home as late as three or four in the morning. He was very gay as well as "handsomer and stouter" than ever. At forty-nine, his hair was graying, whereas at fifty-five, Elizabeth's remained dark with a "sprinkling" of gray underneath. The women continued to adore him.

Pen studied music and arithmetic with his father, Latin with the Abbé, and fencing. At twelve, Pen still wore curls and costumes and slept in his parents' room. Looking at him one day, his mother felt a pang as she realized that the curls and cuddling would soon have to go as he grew into manhood. He fraternized with the French troops on the Pincio. The young Queen of Naples noticed him. At a *matinée d'enfants* at the French Embassy, he chatted about ponies and Chopin with young Italian princes.

During the Roman spring, Elizabeth went out for a few drives in a carriage. Intrepidly she ventured into the *Caffè Greco* on the Via Condotti, where Mr. Story presented Hans Christian Andersen to her. Mr. Andersen kissed her hand. At the Storys' children's party in the Palazzo Barberini, Hans Andersen recited his "Ugly Duckling." Then Robert recited his own "Pied Piper." Then Story played the flute and led the children in gay procession through the noble rooms.

Elizabeth thought they should go to France during the summer so that Robert could see his father and sister after three years of separation, but he thought she was too weak to go that year. Then she suggested that he and Pen go without her, and again he refused. His plan was to return to Florence and then decide on where to spend the summer, very likely in Siena again.

Casa Guidi
June 5 to June 29, 1861

Elizabeth felt comparatively well after the carriage trip from Rome. On June 6, the day after their arrival in Florence, Cavour died at the age of fifty and "at his zenith." She had not recovered from the news of Henrietta's death six months previously, and this blow left her "beaten and bruised." She never left the house again and was not able to please Robert by taking more than two steps with him on the terrace, although she tried. She felt that she was "only fit for a drag chain" on Robert.

On Thursday evening, June 20, Robert was out at Vieusseux' newsroom. When the windows at Casa Guidi, closed during the day to exclude the suffocating heat, were opened, Elizabeth sat in the cross-draughts. After Robert returned, she complained of a sore throat. The next day she had a cold, and Saturday night her cough alarmed him. At one in the morning, he left her with Annunziata and went to get Dr. Wilson. The doctor suspected an abscess in the right lung and prescribed medicine and a slight increase in the morphine.

Every day Robert carried her to her armchair in the drawing room, where she read the newspapers and wrote a few letters. Then a small bed was brought into the drawing room and she lay on that. Friday was the first day she remained in the bedroom, not because she could not get up but because Robert Lytton spent the morning in the drawing room with Robert. That evening Isa Blagden called and thought she had improved, as did Wilson, who called and returned to her own house.

At night, Robert sent the servants away and sat by his wife, as he had been doing. She dozed and waked. "Come to bed," she said. She seemed to think she was on a comfortable steamer, and Robert attributed her lightheadedness to the morphine. When some symptoms alarmed him about four on Saturday morning, he awakened Annunziata and sent the porter for the doctor. To please Robert, Elizabeth let him feed her some spoonfuls of "fowl-jelly." She put her arms around him and kissed him vehemently, saying repeatedly, "God bless you." Then she kissed the air and her own hands. She did not ask for Pen, who was in the next room. Robert raised her in his arms as she struggled to cough. When her head fell against him, he thought she had fainted. Annunziata had to tell him. "*Quest' anima benedetta è passata*," she said.

CASA GUIDI

Casa Guidi

The building now known as Casa Guidi was originally two buildings. The first, a *casa* or house rather than a *palazzo* or *1* palace, occupied the angle formed by the juncture of the Via Maggio and the Via Mazzetta, specifically that portion that includes the first five windows from the corner on the Via Mazzetta. This house was begun in the fifteenth century (as was the Pitti Palace) by the Ridolfi family, who wanted a residence near the Pitti. Luca Pitti had hoped to surpass the Medici in the grandeur of his palace but had to discontinue its construction after he lost his power struggle with the Medici in the year 1466. The abrupt discontinuance of the rusticated stone on the face of the Ridolfi *casa* suggests that they, too, had to retrench. The Medici acquired the palace through marriage, and in 1550 the Pitti Palace rather than the Palazzo Vecchio became the residence of the reigning sovereign. In 1618, Count Camillo Guidi, Secretary of State for the Medici Grand Dukes Francesco I and Cosimo II, bought the corner house from Lorenzo Ridolfi. (He was the Count Guidi who made the diplomatic arrangements for the marriage in 1600 of Maria de' Medici to Henry IV of France.)

The second house, now an extension of the first, belonged to a Commenda of the Military Order of Saint Stephen, and as such was given in 1650 to Admiral Camillo Guidi, a nephew of Count Camillo. In the eighteenth century, both houses became the property of the Guidi family and were unified. The unification included the construction of a new entrance and staircase, the erection of the terrace overlooking the Via Mazzetta, and the decorating of magnificent reception rooms on the *piano nobile* or first floor.

In the 1840's, the Guidi considered selling the house, for they had other residences in Florence and environs where they could live and entertain. Upon consideration, their agent decided to rent the building sub-divided into apartments. The seventeen rooms of the *piano nobile* were divided into two apartments rented at first with the Guidi furniture and then unfurnished.

The Brownings occupied six of these seventeen rooms, plus pantry and entrance hall. For three months in 1847 (from July 20 to October 19), they rented the apartment with the Guidi furniture, which included "satin couches," "marble consoles," "carved & gilt arm chairs, all in crimson & white satin," "noble mirrors," and plate elegant enough to entertain royalty. On May 9 of the next year they took possession of the same rooms unfurnished and acquired their own furniture. Thereafter, they renewed the lease annually until Elizabeth's death in June of 1861. For the furnished rooms they paid a guinea a week; for the rooms unfurnished they paid twenty-five guineas a year. Amenities included admission to the Boboli Gardens and the services of the porter. He lodged near the front door, lighted visitors up the dark stairway to the tenants' apartments, and carried the water that the Browning household required every day.

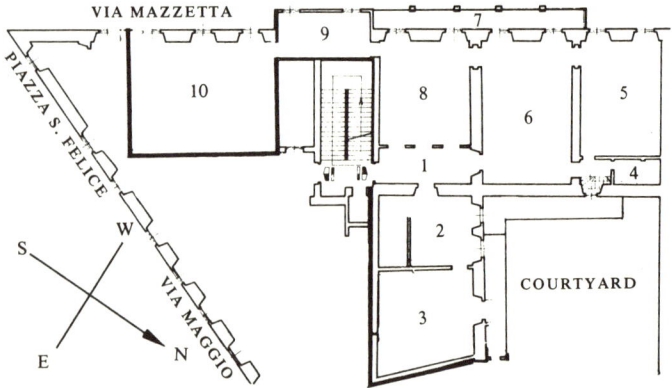

15   Floor plan of Casa Guidi.

1. Entrance Hall

The entrance hall, which leads into the drawing room, remains the same as during the poets' occupancy, with the stained glass partition on the visitor's left dividing it from the dining room. They covered the floor with cane matting.

2. Maid's Room

This room was originally partitioned into a bedroom and sitting room for the maid, the furnishings including an iron bedstead curtained with white muslin. Maid Elizabeth Wilson lived in these rooms until 1857, when, two years after her marriage to the Brownings' man-servant, she moved into a house of her own one door away from Casa Guidi.

3. Nursery

Robert used this area as his dressing room until the birth of his son, Pen, on March 9, 1849. Then it became Pen's nursery. The elegant bedstead had muslin curtains and gilt ornaments for the bedposts. A "high stove" supplied heat, and the French window opened on the courtyard terrace on which Pen kept his pet rabbits. The man-servant also lodged in this area. (A sketch of the apartment that Mrs. Browning made for her sister Arabel in a letter dated May 10–11, 1848, shows a partition in Room 2 and no partition in Room 3.)

4. Kitchen

This room is more properly a butler's pantry, but the servants boiled and broiled, and baked, and roasted full meals in it. (The Guidi kitchen, which the Brownings did not rent, was, as was typical of large Italian houses, on the ground floor.) The ceilings of the *piano nobile* were so high that this pantry was subdivided into two levels, the upper level or loft being reached by "a sort of ladder staircase." A covered passage from the maid's room allowed servants access to the kitchen without passing through the hall and drawing room. This passage has since been converted into a terrace, and the present staircase to the kitchen loft blocks the entrance from the former passageway. A door from this area opens into the Brownings' bedroom and another into the drawing room.

5. Bedroom

3 When the poets began furnishing the apartment in the spring of 1848, they removed the old Guidi carpeting and discovered that the floor underneath was "all in scagliola" and that "the arms of the Counts Guidi" were "blazoned there in many colors." In the autumn they installed new carpeting. Their bed was "of ducal size" with spring mattress, down pillows, and white muslin curtains. On the wall opposite the bed, they hung a portrait of Elizabeth's father. When Pen was seven and a half (1856), they bought a new child's bed for him, and he afterwards slept at the foot of his parents' bed instead of in the nursery, which remained his territory for daytime use. The first piece of furniture they bought was a chest of drawers of "walnut inlaid with ivory" that had belonged to the Guidi and remained in the bedroom. Other furniture in this room included two sofas, a "great" wardrobe, a looking glass, a washing stand, and other chests. Yet the large "palace" room was not crowded. The two windows were curtained in white muslin with crimson tops. On cold nights, Robert tended the fire in the stove and made coffee on it whenever Elizabeth was ill, as she often was. In this room, Pen was born and Elizabeth died.

6. Drawing Room

2 This room measures twenty by thirty-three feet, and the ceilings of all the rooms are "immensely high." Here Elizabeth wrote her letters and poetry, and the poets received their visitors. Elizabeth wrote, "The walls are green, the chairs crimson, with white & gold frames, & the carpet mixes up all the colours. The ceiling has a good deal of gilding in Italian fashion."

Kate Field, a young American friend, described the room as it appeared during her frequent visits between 1859 and 1861. "There was something about this room," she wrote, "that seemed to make it a proper and especial haunt for poets. The dark shadows and subdued light gave it a dreamy look, which was enhanced by the tapestry-covered walls and the old pictures of saints that looked out sadly from their carved frames of black wood. Large bookcases, constructed of specimens of Florentine carving selected by Mr. Browning, were brimming over with wise-looking books. Tables were covered with more gayly bound volumes, the gifts of brother authors. Dante's grave profile, a cast of Keats's face and brow taken after death, a pen-and-ink sketch of Tennyson, the genial face of John Kenyon, Mrs. Browning's good friend and relative, little paintings of the boy Browning, all attracted the eye in turn, and gave rise to a thousand musings. A quaint mirror, easy-chairs and sofas, and a hundred nothings that always add an indescribable charm, were all massed in this room. But the glory of all, and that which sanctified all, was seated in a low arm-chair near the door. A small table, strewn with writing-materials, books, and newspapers, was always by her side."

George Mignaty's painting of the drawing room, done at Robert's request soon after Elizabeth's death, is reproduced as frontispiece. See also the schematic chart on page 97, under which the furnishings are described in detail.

7. Terrace

There is access to the long, narrow terrace through the four windows of the drawing room and dining room. Because the **4** poets missed having a garden, they planned from the first to fill the terrace with plants and trees. In the spring of 1857, the terrace was "green with quite high trees – daturas & others," and the smell of lemon blossoms came through the open windows. That same autumn, the datura trees were covered with "great white lilies, almost like the Victoria lily," and the lemon tree had two ripening lemons. As the poets walked arm in arm on the terrace, they enjoyed the music of the choir and organ of the Church of San Felice across the street. By looking "sideways" from the terrace, they could see "the least tip of the Boboli trees against the sky."

8. Dining Room

The sideboard, which had come from a convent in Urbino, was one hundred years old with carved "figures at the sides, old men's heads for handles & locks of gilt bronze." On the dining-room table was "a little spit of French construction which is wound up like a watch." The tops of the windows were "of crimson imitation of damask," and each red curtain was crossed "with another of the white muslin (cornices carved & gilt.)" The room was heated by a small fireplace.

9. Sitting Room

The "little sitting room at the end of the suite" was "very prettily furnished," and Robert used it after Pen's birth as a dressing room, though he did not like "to throw coats & waistcoats about in it." Until his own studio (Room 10) was furnished, he worked here, and it is in this room that he wrote much of *Men and Women*. Elizabeth mentions "a cloud of angels" looking down from the ceiling.

4

10. Studio

The original lease did not include this room, which the Brownings acquired when they renewed their lease on May 1, 1850. Elizabeth wrote, "They have given us another room in this house, opening out of Robert's dressing room – an enormous room with three great windows; for which we pay two pounds a year more." It was not carpeted and furnished until 1856, when it became Robert's "dressing room, studio & writing room in one." In it he had "crowds of casts & artistic machinery," and mannikins, as well as a human skeleton to assist him in his study of anatomy. (This room is not now owned by The Browning Institute.)

★

During the last years of their occupancy, the Brownings converted the "little sitting room" (9) into the "little dining room," which was large enough to accommodate the family and their few dinner guests. They also moved the pianoforte from the drawing room (6) to the dining room (8), which guests thereafter used as an anteroom while waiting to be received.

The Drawing Room Furnishings

Below is a picture of the drawing room at Casa Guidi based upon the painting by George Mignaty (see frontispiece) and the catalogue of *The Browning Collections* sold at auction by Sotheby in London in 1913. Figures in parentheses ( ) give the prices that the Brownings paid at time of purchase, and the figures in brackets [ ] tell the prices the items brought at the auction.

☐ **A** *Christ at the Column*, with landscapes and with figures of saints in the background. On old Italian panel. 2 ft. 6 in. by 2 ft.*
Browning thought this painting to be by Antonio Pollaiuolo and mentions it in his "Old Pictures in Florence," stanza xxvii. It is now in Harewood House.

[£500]

☐ **B** A tall-back carved wood settee, plush upholstered.
(£2)   [£15.10]

☐ **C** An open-fronted carved wood bookcase.

[£15]

☐ **D** An artist of the Tuscan school, Center of triptych: *Crucifixion*, framed. four side wings: single figures of male and female saints, unframed. On old Italian panels.

[£36]

☐ **E** Ridolfo del Ghirlandaio (1483–1561), *The Eternal Father*, altar piece with God the Father as center and an angel on

---

* Measurements of the pictures do not include the frames.

16 *Salon at Casa Guidi* (1861) by George Mignaty. (See also cover.)

17　A schematic drawing of Mignaty's painting.

each side. On old Italian panel. Center panel, 3 ft. 6 in. by 3 ft.; sides 26 in. by 21 in.

(£2.4.6)   [£23]

☐ F A large carved wood gilt mirror, the frame of scroll design, with two amorini at the sides, each supporting two candle branches. 4 ft. 8 in. high by 4 ft. 2 in. wide.

(£5)   [£7]

☐ G Tuscan School, *Portrait of a Bishop*. 16 in. by 11 in.

[see H]

☐ H *The Penitent St. Jerome*, a full-length figure of the saint standing with hand to his breast, his cardinal's hat at his feet. 20 in. by 14 in. Browning thought this picture was by Taddeo Gaddi and mentions it in his "Old Pictures in Florence," stanza xxvi. It is now at Princeton University, attributed to Giovanni Toscani, and dated between 1426 and 1430.

[£19 for G & H]

☐ J Two *Busts of a Man and a Woman*, in circular ebonized and gilt frames, 14 in. in diameter. These were greatly admired by John Ruskin.

[£5.10]

☐ K A large wood bookcase with brass diamond panelled screen and carved angels, serpents, and infants.

(£6)   [£65]

☐ L An Italian ebonized table with inlaid ebony and ivory top and spirally fluted legs. 2 ft. 3 in. high by 3 ft. 7 in. by 2 ft. 4 in.

[£6.16]

☐ M A North Italian walnut table, with marquetry shaped top and bowed legs. 2 ft. 5 in. high by 3 ft. 6 in. by 2 ft. 4 in.

[£5.10]

☐ N A North Italian walnut marquetry topped table, with ebonized spirally fluted legs. 2 ft. 4 in. high by 4 ft. 1 in. by 2 ft. 1 in.

[£3.7.6]

☐ **O** A deep back plush upholstered arm chair. Elizabeth called this "her" chair and thought it "most luxurious."

[£100]

☐ **P** A lady's maple-wood work table, with center pedestal, on four feet, the top painted with a landscape in oils and ornamental corner pieces, fitted with one drawer. 25 in. high by 21 in. by 15 in. This was Elizabeth's work table. It also stood in Robert's study at his two London houses, and is shown in a drawing by Felix Moschelles.

[£25.10]

☐ **Q** A folding deck arm chair with plain slats. This was Elizabeth's chair.

[£22.10]

☐ **R** Elizabeth's writing case with sloping lid, in dark blue leather, tooled with gold. Robert and Pen kept this writing case just as it was on the day she died. At the auction it still contained her bead-work purse, a miniature portrait of Napoleon III, two small inkstands, and three numbers of the Italian newspaper *La Nazione*, which continued to be delivered for three days after her death.

[£23.10]

☐ **S** A mahogany writing table, the center of the top opening and forming a writing slant, turned legs and stretchers, fitted with one drawer. 2 ft. 3 in. high by 2 ft. 5 in. by 17 in.

[£24]

☐ **T** An Italian ebonized table, with inlaid ebony and ivory top, spirally fluted legs, 2 ft. 3 in. high by 3 ft. 7 in. by 2 ft. 4 in.

[£7.10]

AFTERWORD

Elizabeth

Elizabeth Barrett Browning (March 6, 1806–June 29, 1861) was buried on Monday, July 1, at seven in the evening in the Protestant Cemetery in Florence. The services were conducted by the chaplain of the English church, because Robert wanted to hear "those only words at the beginning" of the English burial service, even though in Florence she had worshipped with the Dissenters. Shops on the Via Maggio were closed during the service, and men wept. In 1862, the City of Florence placed a memorial tablet over the entrance to Casa Guidi. Robert dedicated Elizabeth's posthumous *Last Poems* to the City of Florence and to Niccolò Tommaseo, the poet who had composed the inscription. In 1865, after many delays, her monument was erected in the cemetery. Designed by Frederic Leighton, the monument consists of a sarcophagus supported by six pillars. The central medallion represents an idealized head of Poetry.

In 1897, the publication of two volumes of her letters was of major literary importance. Robert was opposed to the publication of letters and burnt any number in his possession. He planned to destroy their love letters, which he kept in an inlaid box, but he never could bring himself to burn these. In 1899, Pen allowed them to be published in two volumes. In 1930, *The Barretts of Wimpole Street*, a play by Rudolf Besier, popularized the love story.

Robert

Robert Browning (May 7, 1812–December 12, 1889) took from Elizabeth's finger a gold ring Isa Blagden had given her, and he wore it on his watch chain for the twenty-eight years he survived his wife. He left Florence on August 1, 1861, never to return. He became a social lion in London and was honored with degrees by Oxford, Cambridge, and the University of Edinburgh and by the founding of the Browning Society in his lifetime. He always believed Elizabeth to be the better poet, loved her always, and had no doubt that he would join her after death. (Nevertheless, he felt obliged to assert that he had been proved right and she wrong on all points on which they had disagreed.) On one of his trips to Venice, he died at the age of seventy-seven in Pen's house there and was buried in Westminster Abbey.

Pen

Robert Wiedeman Barrett Browning (March 9, 1849–July 8, 1912) had his curls cut off and boy's clothes substituted for his fantastic dress within a week of his mother's death. He was tutored privately for Oxford, where he matriculated at Christ Church but failed after three terms. He then went to the Continent to study painting and sculpture, the latter under Rodin, and he exhibited in the best of the London and Paris galleries. In 1887, he married an American heiress and purchased one of the finest palaces in Venice, the Palazzo Rezzonico, which he furnished impressively. After Robert's death, Pen's wife left him and became an Anglican nun. He remained in Italy, reverted to fantastic clothes, dressed like a Paris jockey, and loved the company of his inferiors. He died and was buried in Asolo, near Venice. Ten years later, his wife had his body removed to Florence, where he and his Aunt Sarianna are buried in the new Protestant Cemetery.

Wilson

Elizabeth Wilson Romagnoli (1820–1902) looked after Walter Savage Landor until his death in 1864, when her business failed. She returned to England, set up a lodging house in Scarborough, and again failed. She returned to Italy destitute, and Robert allowed her £10 a year. Her son Oreste joined her in Florence in the summer of 1862, when he was almost seven, and her son Pilade died in Florence in 1878 at the age of twenty. When Pen purchased the Palazzo Rezzonico, he took her there, and she lived with him until her death in Asolo, where she is buried. Fifty years after her death, she was still remembered as Pen's nurse, old and crazy, *piccola – piccola*, roaming over the hills near Asolo, alone.

Ferdinando

Ferdinando Romagnoli (1819–1893) helped Wilson to care for Landor after Robert and Pen left Florence. In 1885, Robert rediscovered him in Venice working as a cook for an American family, who valued "his honesty and culinary cleverness." Pen took him to live in the Rezzonico, and he stayed with his "bosom friend" until his death.

The Furnishings

After attempts at photography proved unsatisfactory, Robert had his friend George Mignaty paint a picture of the drawing room as it was at the time of Elizabeth's death. Then the furniture, books, tapestries, and pictures were packed in crates and stored. A year later the furnishings were delivered to the London house that Robert rented. After his death, the furniture went to Pen in Italy, and after Pen's death all was sold at auction in London at Sotheby's, May 1–8, 1913.

Casa Guidi

In 1893, Pen tried to go home again by purchasing the building with the intention of returning the furnishings to their old places in his parents' apartment. After his death, the building was bought by Mrs. Ellen Laura Hutchinson Centaro, an American from Georgia, who in 1916 mounted the memorial tablet on the Via Mazzetta side of the building. In 1971, the Browning Institute purchased the Brownings' apartment from the Centaro heirs with the purpose of refurnishing the poets' rooms and maintaining them as a memorial and study center.

THE BROWNINGS' FLORENCE

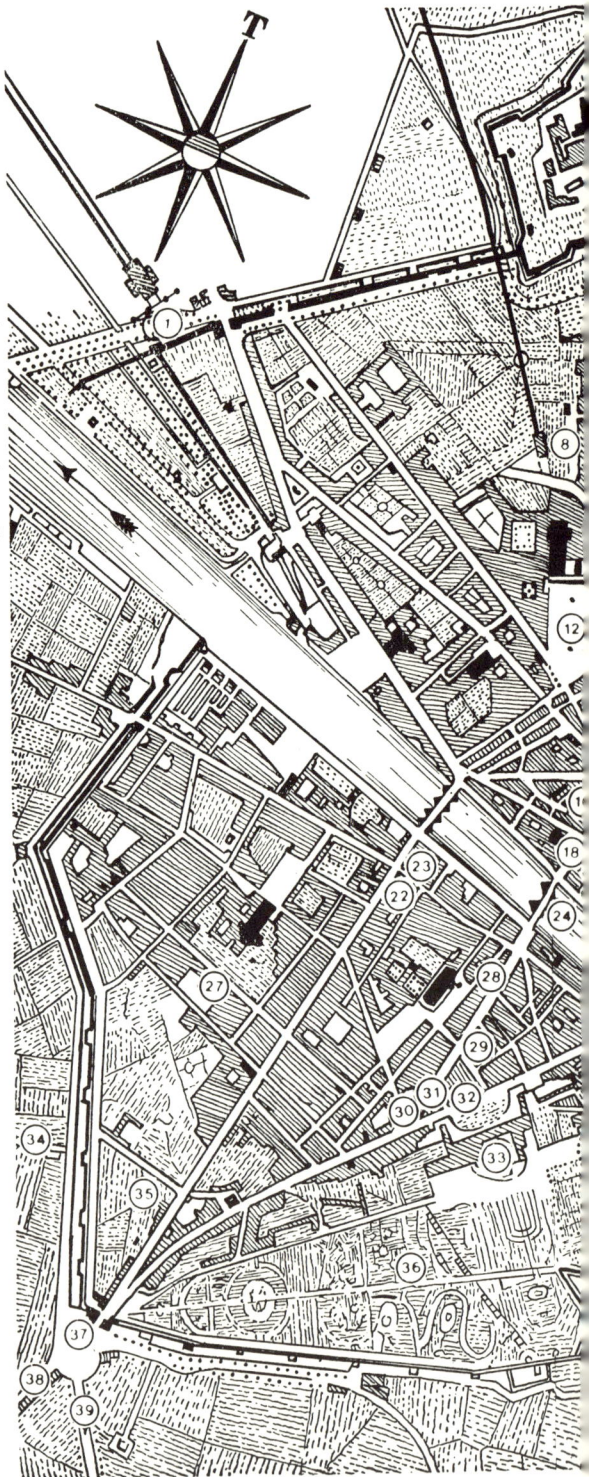